The Yankee Chick's
Survival Guide to Texas

T0159247

Sophia Dembling

REPUBLIC OF TEXAS PRESS

Dallas • Lanham • Boulder • New York • Toronto • Plymouth, UK

Published by Republic of Texas Press
An imprint of The Rowman & Littlefield Publishing Group, Inc.
4501 Forbes Boulevard, Suite 200
Lanham, MD 20706

Estover Road
Plymouth PL6 7PY
United Kingdom

Distributed by NATIONAL BOOK NETWORK

ISBN 10: 1-55622-888-0
ISBN 13: 978-1-55622-888-9

⊖™ The paper used in this publication meets the minimum requirements of American National Standard for Information Sciences—Permanence of Paper for Printed Library Materials, ANSI/NISO Z39.48-1992

Manufactured in the United States of America.

For Tom

with everlasting love and appreciation

Contents

Acknowledgments

My deepest gratitude goes to the Yankee chicks who so generously shared their opinions, observations, anecdotes, and insights about our adopted home. This book would be nothing without them. I used no last names in order to permit total candor, but they know who they are. Thanks again to: Andrea, Anne, Barbara, Beth, Cerie, Dana, Ellen, Ginnie, Holly, Jennifer, Joyce, Judy, Karen, Karen, Kim, Kim, Laura, Linda, Linda, Lisa, Lucy, Maggie, Maria, Mary, Melanie, Melanie, Pam, Pat, Rett, and Tara.

Special thanks to Ginnie Bivona for making my first book finally happen, and to Linda Crosson for reading the whole darn thing at a thoroughly inconvenient time and liking it anyway. Thanks to Nancy Kruh, who has helped shape me as a writer; to Mary Jacobs, for resisting the impulse to pop me in the nose while she helped me figure things out; to Dave Baumbach for taking on the scary task of reading early drafts; and to John Anders, Jenny Owen, and Christine Wicker for their support, encouragement, suggestions, insights, and friendship.

September 11, 2001

The writing of this book was completed shortly before the devastating events of September 11, 2001.

Watching New York City, my hometown, in such duress from so far away was painful in a manner too intense and personal to discuss here. I am deeply grateful to my Texan friends who reached out to me in compassion. The pain we have felt has been shared as Americans and individually, as each of us processed the inconceivable events in our own ways. Shortly after the attacks, I spoke to a couple of the Yankee chicks quoted in this book, and all of us felt the same strange compulsion to run "home." (Where is home? Is it where you hang your hat, where the heart is, or both?)

I agonized over the decision of releasing the book so soon after the attacks. After all, the nation is seeking unity and the book describes differences. In addition, Texans have felt unusually tender towards New Yorkers since that terrible day and might take extra offense at having their previous ambivalence towards Yankees revealed now.

I decided to proceed for nebulous reasons: Because I could not predict how anyone would feel on the day that the book hit the shelves. Because despite the affection the nation suddenly feels for its greatest city (in my biased opinion), this does not change the cultural differences I discuss here. And because in these complicated, confusing times, Yankee chicks in Texas, like myself, may be feeling more homesick and far from home than ever. This book is for them, to help them understand their adopted home. Perhaps, too, Texans will read this book and glean deeper understanding of their Yankee neighbors, and the warmth that tragedy inspired will grow and blossom into something deep and lasting.

Introduction

Yankee's Apology

Texans will probably hate this book.

Don't misunderstand: I didn't set out to write a book that Texans will hate and I'm not thrilled that they will. But I am not only a Yankee in Texas, I am the most heinous of Yankees: a New Yorker. As such, there is no way I could say anything about Texas—other than "WOW, IT'S THE BEST PLACE EVER!" —without pissing Texans off.

When I showed some early pages of the book to my editor, she was appalled by some of my observations. "How can you say these things about Texas?" she said. "You've been here what, twenty years? You're a Texan!" Moments later, with equal heat, she said, "You're not allowed to say these things about Texas! You're not a Texan!"

This is the transplanted Yankee's predicament in a nutshell. We're no longer Yankees. We're not Texans. No matter how long we have lived here, if we were born in Yankeeland we're carpetbaggers and nobody asked for our opinion, thank you very much. Soon I will have lived in Texas as long as I lived in New York. But my decades in Texas are well below admissions requirement for being considered a Texan. New Yorkers grumble that you can step off the bus from Podunk and call yourself a New Yorker that day. In Texas, the requirement I've heard is five generations on Texas soil. By that standard, I'm not even an American. I'm only second generation at that.

I have no family or history in Texas, and compared with a real Texan, my roots here are still thin as the hairs on a freshly pulled carrot. Nonetheless, Texas is my home. I can think of a million things—from people I've come to depend on to the way the sky looks after a rain—that I would miss if I moved away. Texas has been very, very good to me, and as much as I have found my place in it, it has also taken a place within me.

But though I love Texas, it is like the love you might feel for an old friend's husband. You might think he's the best thing since salsa but still be far less likely than his wife to chuckle indulgently if he emits a window-rattling belch at the dinner table. Texans in love with their state not only chuckle indulgently at such dubious behavior, they staunchly defend the right of an individual to belch at his own table and invite any guests who might be bothered to simply take their Emily-la-di-da-Post asses home.

In a way, I admire the sentiment. People should stand up for what they believe in, and I agree that a man has the right to rattle the windows at his own dinner table. However, I would like to think that whether or not he should is a matter open to discussion. Texans, for the most part, don't want to hear about it. So I'm sticking my neck out with this book.

Anything I say about Texas will be taken as a deep affront by some Texans, and they will denounce me roundly. It's a pity, since I'm not out to make enemies. Texans like to boast that they're different from Yankees, and Yankees, for the most part, agree. So what's the big argument? The Yankees and Texans who get along best are the ones who know how to bridge those differences. I'm sorry that Texans are going to be angry at me, but Texas is changing. The Yankees are definitely coming. And coming. And coming. And we're not going home, so we might as well all learn to get along.

Chapter One

When Culture Shocks

*"I've handled the Middle East.
I can handle Texas."*

— *Anne, Maryland, two years in Texas*

*T*he first thing to know is that in Texas, the term "Yankee" has little to do with the Civil War (a.k.a. the War of Northern Aggression). Certainly there are those with Confederate flags on their pickup trucks who still hold a grudge about "the great unpleasantness," wielding it in indignant letters to the editor from time to time. But for the purposes of this book—and as the reality of life down here—"Yankee" is a loose term covering a lot of ground. A woman at my friend Barbara's bank called her a "damn Yankee" when she went to open her first account. "I thought, 'But Oregon didn't fight in the Civil War,'" Barbara recalls. Anne, who moved from Maryland, tries to object. "First of all, I am a die-hard Orioles fan," she says. "I am not a Yankee. Yankees play in Yankee stadium."

Too bad. If you're not a Texan or a southerner, you're a Yankee.

The East Coast is a hotbed of Yankees, of course. But so is the West Coast. Californians are Yankees, and Chicagoans. There are Yankees from Cleveland and from Des Moines. Basically, if you come from anywhere vaguely north of the Mason-Dixon line you're a Yankee and therefore, to many Texans, suspect. "Well, I've never known a Yankee I liked," a Texan drawled at Judy, shortly after she moved from New York thirteen years ago.

It's been a long time since I've spotted the bumper sticker "Love NY? Take I-30 East," Texans' last gasp protest against the last flood of Yankees. They were common when I moved to Texas in 1982. Texans only barely tolerated Yankees back then, when we rode down in droves on the Urban Cowboy craze of the late 1970s and into the early '80s. Talk about carpetbaggers—Texas was rolling in oil wealth and there we suddenly all were, ready to share the riches. When the state's oil-based economy took a big hit in the mid-1980s, Texans watched with disgust as Yanks who hurried down for the good times hurried right back up when the money wells ran dry. I arrived in the waning days of Texas oil prosperity and stayed through the bust, a leftover Yankee among a disgruntled and disappointed tribe of natives putting the state back together. Now Texas is booming again and Yankees are streaming back in, some with enthusiasm, others reluctantly following their jobs or their spouses' jobs. High tech and corporate relocations have brought new flocks of Yankees down, and they're finding that Texas offers an ease of living that's hard to walk away from. Today the bumper sticker reads: "I wasn't born in Texas but I got here as fast as I could."

There are many rites of passage to being a Yankee in Texas. The first time you spot a pickup with a gun rack. Your first "Jesus Loves You" billboard. The first time someone calls you a Yankee. The first time you realize that a week is a long time to go without Mexican food. The first time you recognize a change in the season. Your first thunderstorm. Your first honky-tonk.

And then there are the moments that reveal beyond any doubt that the differences here run deeper than cowboy boots with business suits.

I had my epiphany buying matzo in my local supermarket. Matzo, a pantry staple for many in my hometown of New York City, was not common in Dallas stores in the early eighties. Back then it appeared mostly around Passover, and I always bought it when I found it. So there I was one spring day, at the supermarket with my box of matzo. As the checker rang up groceries for the woman ahead of me in line, she accidentally picked up my matzo. The customer took one look at the Hebrew lettering on the box and, terror in her eyes, grabbed the checker's arm. "That's not mine," she said. "I don't know *what* it is, but it's *not mine!*"

Man, I thought. Where am I?

Every Texas transplant has a moment like that. For Melanie from Maryland, it was when as a newspaper reporter, she called a city bureau to get information on gun permits. "The woman said, 'Ma'am this is Texas. You don't have to have a permit to carry a gun,'" she recalls. "I just kept saying 'What?' She had to repeat herself several times." For Pam from New York, it was when she called utilities companies to set up accounts. "They couldn't understand me and I couldn't understand them," she says. Linda from Pennsylvania says, "I asked the guy at the supermarket seafood counter for lox . . . well, you can imagine . . . ."

And once, a couple of years after I arrived in Texas, I stood right next to the late Tom Landry in a Baskin Robbins. He was wearing the hat and everything. The guy I was with—an educated and cultured native Texan—was goggle-eyed as a schoolboy and appalled to learn after the Great One left the store that I hadn't even noticed. I was equally horrified to find myself in the company of someone who got starry-eyed around a football coach.

Then there are the times you realize that not only are you far from home, but you're something of an oddity yourself. For Melanie from New Jersey it was when she said something innocuous in front of a group of people and they all burst out laughing.

We've all had that experience.

"Oh," they finally say, wiping away tears. "You sound so *Yankee.*"

For Melanie, the word was *"aw*-fice." For me, it was "sneakers.*"* (Down here they're "tennis shoes.")

Until moments like these, you might not have even realized you were a Yankee. But you are. Now and forever, even if you live in Texas until you draw your last breath.

When I was growing up, most of my friends, like me, had heavily accented relatives of one sort or another—Polish, Italian, Puerto Rican. We were all loosely planted in American soil. Here in Texas, I have one friend who shares a name with the East Texas town her ancestors founded. The other day at a charity event, I met a very nice college-age lad whose ancestors were among the original 300 settlers of Texas. My neighbor and her late husband built their home when what is now an urban neighborhood was all pastureland, and a major street a few blocks away is named for a member of her family. Another friend owns a West Texas ranch from which his granddaddy (granddaddy—a word I never would have used pre-Texas) cowboyed around the turn of the century. True Texans are woven into the state by generations. I scarcely imagined people like this existed, much less that I would encounter them in regular old life.

And unlike the loose roots of port cities, Texans don't often move far from Texas. If they do, they don't stay away long. It's not unusual to meet people who live just blocks from their childhood homes, or even in their childhood homes. The truest Texans gain psychic nourishment from the state. Everyone who lives in Texas and followed the television show *Survivor* in 2001 understood Texan contestant Colby, who took the Texas flag as one of only two personal items he was allowed to carry to the Outback. It is impossible to imagine anyone taking the Illinois flag, the Vermont flag, or even the New York flag, just as it is impossible to imagine anyone making Christmas cookies in the shape of California. Texans are bound to their state in a million ways, from family history to the visceral need for wide-open spaces and boundless optimism.

Texans' devotion to their home state is as endearing as it is infuriating. I can only admire that sort of passion, and it is among the reasons I chose Texas as my new home. It was important to me that Texans are as passionate about Texas as New Yorkers are about New York. In a way, Texans and New Yorkers are similar. They both believe they inhabit the center of the universe and pity the fools who choose to live elsewhere. Yet love doth not a Texan make.

If I respond "Dallas" when people ask where I'm from, the next question is invariably, "No, where are you *really* from?" Yankees in Texas learn to say, "I *live in* Texas" rather than "I'm *from* Texas." It's more accurate, no matter how long you've had a Texas ZIP code. So, if not a Texan, could I still be a New Yorker? Surely there's a statute of limitations on that. But then, what am I? That's a question on which I have pondered long and hard, to conclude that I haven't the faintest idea. The only time I ever feel even remotely Texan is when I'm in New York and realize that I speak and move more slowly than my old friends; I don't have quite the tolerance for bitching and moaning I once did (though I certainly enjoy it more than Texans); and all the TV newscasters sound like Rhoda Morgenstern. Also, after a week in The City (as New Yorkers think of it), I have lost all patience with crowds and can't wait to get back to the wide-open spaces of Dallas.

But no matter how I feel, as a Yankee, I can't pass. "I walk fast, I talk fast. True Texans can usually spot me," says Rett, who moved down twelve years ago from New Jersey. Even standing still, I seem to exude Yankeeness in ways I can't pinpoint. Are my clothes too dark? Is my gaze too direct? Are my fingernails too ragged? (Yes.) Or are people able to look deep into my soul and see that I don't understand exactly why the Alamo is considered a shrine? (Now that I've said that, lavender-haired ladies in San Antonio are clutching their chests and Bubba is reaching for his concealed handgun to escort me to the border.)

Yankees in Texas blend but don't melt. To gather information for this book, I talked to Yankee chicks who moved to Texas as recently as a year ago and as long as fifty years ago. While long-timers like me were certainly more at ease with Texas ways than the newcomers, there was no one among the women who didn't have something to say about culture shock, the way Texas had changed them, the way they would change Texas if they could. (Actually, having something to say about nearly everything is a quintessentially Yankee trait that we learn to suppress in Texas.) After years of being told that nobody wants to hear what they have to say about Texas, inviting Yankee chicks to open up on the subject, with license to gripe if necessary, caused an explosion of commentary, some harsh, some affectionate, some just befuddled. When I gathered a group of Yankee chicks together for bagels and lox for a Yankee chick chat in my living room, we had moments where the comment of one brought whoops of relieved recognition from the rest of us. All our years of navigating Texas society without a map exploded in several hours of bitching, venting, laughing, healthy Yankee disagreements, and a symphony of

honking accents. We were from Iowa, New York, Massachusetts, New Jersey, Ohio, California, Pennsylvania, and
Missouri, but we understood each other perfectly. To be able to
say out loud, "So what's with football?" and have a room full of
women throw their hands in the air and roll their eyes was liberating. And when one Yankee Chick said, "I knew I was in the
right place when I saw the cars parked out front," we all looked
out the window at a row of small, beaten-down old cars and felt
not the shame a Texan would feel driving a jalopy the size of a
pedal car, but good, frugal, Yankee pride. Texas changed us
all—some more than others—but we still shared a bond and
knew from whence we came. After a couple of hours of discussion about clothes, church, education, guns, food, women, men,
and more, the Yankee chicks were all slumped in their seats
looking spent, exhausted, purged.

Culture shock in Texas can be intense and it is exacerbated
by local rules of propriety that tell us to keep our mouths shut.
But here, in this book, we are going to talk about it all, with
good old Yankee outspokenness. We'll clear the air, share
experiences, orient newcomers, and generally get it out of our
systems because the more we understand, the easier it will be
to assimilate. As we grow accustomed to Texas's eccentrici-
ties, Yankee chicks appreciate the better points of the lifestyle.
Texans have a hearty appreciation of *joie de vivre*, although they
would never call it that or if they did they would probably mis-
pronounce it. Yankees who stay in Texas are those who have
come to appreciate that appreciation.

"Twenty-five years from now, you'll feel about Texas the
way I do," said Uncle Bawley to newcomer Elizabeth Taylor in
Giant. Now, we might never feel exactly the way a Texan does.
(Or maybe we will. Who knows?) But Texas is different. The

happiest transplants are those who don't expect to simply transfer their old lives to this new location. To move to Texas is to enter a proud and complex culture. If you try to make it what it isn't, you will chafe. If you appreciate what Texas has been, is now, and can be, it will change you in ways you can't even imagine when you first arrive. As one-time candidate for Texas governor Clayton Williams said (effectively ending his political hopes in a most delicious and quintessentially Texas way), if it's inevitable, you might as well relax and enjoy it.

Homework

Much of what the world thinks it knows of Texas comes from how it is depicted in literature, movies, and television. Some of the depictions hit the mark, some don't. Among my favorites.

Lonesome Dove: This is one of the few books written about Texas that Texans didn't hate before they loved it—it is the true Texan's favorite book. Larry McMurtry's epic Pulitzer Prize-winning tale of a cattle drive is Texas the way they want us to see it. So much cowboy literature is John Wayne on paper—dashing, but simplistic—that McMurtry's three-dimensional tale of dirt, death, emotion, and sex is like scratching an itch. "Here!" Texans say. "Here is what we were like, riding and fighting and shooting and loving and feeling, even if we didn't talk about it. We were scared and filthy and sometimes ign'r'nt, but we were brave and loyal and real." Full of danger and adventure, peopled by men of few words and the sturdy, sexy women who love them, the book also is permeated with a sense of longing for something that is slipping away. And don't be put off because it's a Western. It's the best Western ever, the über western. Hang in through the first 100 pages, and you will then have to cancel all plans in order to keep reading straight through to the end.

The Last Picture Show: Larry McMurtry's novel about a small Texas town was not warmly received by the natives, since it lifted a curtain on small town Texas life and revealed sex, cruelty, homosexuality, and other things that definitely do not exist in small towns. But thirty-five years later, the characters seem less horrifying than human and the story feels archetypal. One reason to love McMurtry is because his novels are populated with fully realized, complicated, and compelling female characters. And he

addresses Texas—the state and the state of mind—without hyperbole, with clarity.

Texasville, the sequel to *The Last Picture Show* is not the gem of its predecessor, but it does paint a believable (if slapstick) picture of one Texas town at the moment the bottom dropped out of oil prices. *Dwight's Depressed* was the final book in the trilogy.

Molly Ivins Can't Say That, Can She?: Molly Ivins says whatever she damn well pleases, with wit and style, and this collection of essays is a *de rigueur* introduction to Texas politics. Conservatives may find her annoying, but it's refreshing to have someone speak the unspeakable from time to time. I wonder if she's getting tired of being the token folksy character trotted out nationally when commentary on Texas is required, and I wonder what she'll do if Texas politics ever clean up.

Friday Night Lights: Texans loathed—and still fume over—H.G. Bissinger's look at the phenomenon of the Permian Panthers, a West Texas high school football team. It is most definitely a Yankee's-eye view, but compelling. Just don't tell anyone you're reading it.

Giant: Edna Ferber's novel about West Texas takes place at the moment when ranching was going down and oil was bubbling up. The book annoyed Texans, but they softened after it was made into a glorious classic movie starring James Dean, Rock Hudson, and Elizabeth Taylor. Now Texas embraces the story as its own, especially as the cast and crew all settled in the little town of Marfa for the duration of the filming, and charmed the locals.

The Alamo: The three-hour John Wayne classic is an important nucleus of Texas mythology. (See "Blame John Wayne: The Alamo," page 74.) It's also a ripping yarn.

Hud: With Paul Newman as a surly, sexy cowboy and Patricia Neal as the woman he couldn't seduce, McMurtry's short novel *Horseman, Pass By* was transformed into a screen classic. McMurtry reflects on its place in Texas lore in "Here's HUD in your eye," one of the essays from *In a Narrow Grave*, his excellent collection of essays about Texas.

Urban Cowboy: When John Travolta and Debra Winger hit the dance floor of Gilley's—Mickey Gilley's massive Houston-area honky-tonk—Yankees decided they wanted a piece of that action, too, and suddenly Yankee airwaves were thick with country music radio stations and Texas was full of transplants. The honky-tonk scenes in the film in particular perfectly capture a moment in time.

Dr. T. and the Women: Robert Altman's Dallas tale, starring Richard Gere, Farrah Fawcett, and Laura Dern, is too over the top to be documentary, but it does manage satire and some biting insights into the Dallas head—such as in the city council discussions about naming a freeway for a prominent Dallas woman. (One councilman votes for Jayne Mansfield, born a Yankee but reared in Dallas and perfectly built for the town.) ⬥

Chapter Two

There's No Place Like Home

"*I thought San Antonio would be like West Texas— roadrunners and tumbleweeds. I was kind of disappointed*"

—Anne, Maryland, two years in Texas

*F*ew Yankee chicks have the luxury of selecting where in Texas they want to live. Most of the time they are following job or spouse and must settle for wherever they settle. I am a rare exception—I actually chose Dallas. I chose it, however, because I liked Fort Worth, which, I've since come to understand, was a moronic bit of reasoning. I'd never actually been to Dallas but figured since it was a bigger city, work might be easier to find, and as it was only thirty miles away from Fort Worth—how different could it be? I may have been right about the work part, but in fact, Dallas and Fort Worth are as different as Patty and Cathy, but I didn't learn that until I was thoroughly settled in Dallas. Three years ago my Yankee husband and I found our dream house, and so here we stay.

It's easy to plop yourself down in the wrong place. As soon as they learn they're moving, Yankees hurry down, find a house they fall in love with at a price that makes them giddy (Texas is full of houses like that), and buy it right away, only to discover that they're 40 minutes from any restaurant that isn't part of a chain, living on a street that requires heavy investment in lawn decorations at Christmas (this actually happened to a friend of mine), or in a community where everyone attends the same church.

Anne moved from the East Coast to the sprawling north side of San Antonio and was outta there six months later to settle happily in the inner-city Mahncke Park/Alamo Heights district. "I can walk to IHOP or a little tea shop for Sunday breakfast," she says. "I'm so used to East Coast urban energy. I feed off that and still miss it. This is the area of town where I need to live to retain my sanity."

Laura moved to Texas from Des Moines. "First I moved to the snotty Las Colinas area where everything looks the same, then to the sleepy Lewisville area which is family-land, but I had a house I could afford. Then I moved to the wonderfully eclectic Oak Lawn area. My dog and I don't miss the sound of strollers and Big Wheels."

Karen from Los Angeles moved to Dallas with her boyfriend to be near his family, "But we always knew we would end up in Austin. That's where everyone went to have fun," she said. After five years they did and are thriving in their Austin life of music, organic gardening, and Mexican food.

Joyce moved from Ohio and grabbed an apartment in Carrollton, a Dallas 'burb she hated. She moved into Dallas as soon as her lease was up. (On the other hand, Melanie, who had been living in and loving a hip urban neighborhood in Dallas, bought a house in Carrollton after she had twins and is thrilled with all the space her money could buy in the 'burbs.)

Maria and her husband moved from Seattle to a small town on the Mexican border where they took over his sister's successful Chinese restaurant. "We did very well; this was the spot everyone hung out on weekends," she says. "But the town had only one major street. By 9 p.m. all the lights were off. The only entertainment was a video rental place. I spent thousands in that store." After a year Maria told her husband it was time to move. They now own a sushi restaurant in the affluent Dallas suburb of Plano, which is better, though Maria still yearns for an urban lifestyle. "I want to get out of here, but we have this house my husband adores."

Plano is among the most successful of the many gleaming, fast-growing suburbs springing up all over Texas in areas that, fifteen years ago, were rural. On these huge, unbroken tracts of land one could start from scratch, and so up sprang communities of McMansions fulfilling the dream-house dreams of thousands, and shopping centers of massive proportions, with rows of superstores gleaming in the sun. These are cities with all the character of a brand-new shopping mall. JC Penney relocated its headquarters in Plano when it left New York City in the 1980s. As I understand it, several relocating New Yorkers stepped on Plano soil and immediately burst into flames. You could always recognize new JC Penney transplants when you encountered them. They still wore New York black and they looked very sad. ("The girls from the art department in New York that didn't come with us asked me all sorts of weird questions while I was up there," says one current (Texan) Penney employee. "Like, do we celebrate Christmas in Texas? And aren't there a lot of cults in Texas? They had the idea that it is the Wild West down here—cowboys and Indians and pickup trucks with rednecks and gun racks everywhere.")

Texas's suburbs are mushrooming into small cities themselves, draining urban tax bases while they become self-sufficient, sprawling outward, gobbling up towns in an ever-widening circumference and stitching cities together. Dallas/Fort Worth is called The Metroplex, Midland and Odessa have been joined at the hyphen to become Midland-Odessa. Austin and San Antonio have nearly been connected by suburbs until it's hard to tell where one city's sprawl ends and the other begins. "One sometimes wonders if Bowie and Travis and the rest would have fought so hard for this land if they had known how many ugly motels and shopping centers would eventually stand on it," McMurtry wrote. This phenomenon is not unique to Texas (the East Coast is already one big city, isn't it?), but those of us who have been here a while watch it with dismay. Miles and miles of Texas are turning into miles and miles of shopping and fast food, and our rural state is become citified. "Texans do seem to have a large tolerance for ugly," says Christine, who moved to the Midwest from Texas. "Everyone in my neighborhood thinks our local shopping center is ugly, but I think it's beautiful. It's landscaped and everything."

Moving directly from a Yankee city to a Texas suburb can give you the bends. If you're urban, starting out in a city—even though it's not likely to be of the sort you're used to—helps ease the transition. While Texas cities bear little resemblance to Chicago, Philadelphia, New York, or San Francisco, they do have their own energy, persona, and pace if you can slow down just a little and find it. If you've ever driven on a Houston freeway at rush hour, you will surely recognize the same sort of surly camaraderie in the shared space that one might feel on a New York subway at the end of a work day. When I first moved to Texas, I had to break myself of the habit of saying I was going "to Dallas" when I meant downtown. It's hard for the East Coast urban dweller to understand that even places that look like our idea of the suburbs (single-family homes and lawns) can be inner-city, and that the area of tall buildings is just another neighborhood—one that usually empties out at the end of the work day.

The cities of Texas all have distinct personalities. If you're transplanting yourself to Austin, you hit the jackpot. Yankees love Austin. "...foreigners and easterners surrender their affections to Austin more readily than any other place in the state," McMurtry wrote, clearly not enamored with the city himself. Like the rest of the state, Austin is growing and changing fast and we all gripe about that, but it remains the holy grail of Texas cities—where most urban Texans would live if whatever they do wasn't keeping them where they are. "Austin has a big heart," Ann Richards wrote. "There is an ambiance there that allows you to be whoever you want to be and do whatever you want to do, and the people of Austin will respect your right to do that."

Austin has traditionally been defined by politics (it's the state capital—but you knew that), the University of Texas' nearly 50,000 students, and an equal number of former students who just couldn't tear themselves away. Old Austin is represented by longhair fifty-something guys in Hawaiian shirts who graduated UT in the sixties and never left town. But there's a new Austin muscling in, too, the brash young dot-commers in little webjammer glasses who are taking over Austin while the old hippies hunker down at home listening to Townes Van Zandt and remembering the good old days when you could get across town in less than an hour. But Austin is still in the heart of the Hill Country, and when the city gets wearing you can point your car out of town and soon be in some of the state's prettiest scenery.

Austin is also scene-saturated. It's the center of the Texas music scene, Hollywood for singer-songwriters. It's got the government scene—that whole legislators-with-big-cigars-taking-meetings-at-the-Driskill-Hotel thing. It's got the burnt-orange UT scene. It's got the weekend scene at Barton Springs and the nighttime scene on 6th Street. The "whatever" slacker scene has given way to the driven dot-com scene. Austin is a scene scene. "Groupiness was endemic," McMurtry wrote about Austin. "No one might be missing from the group, lest he turn out to be somewhere better, with a wilder, more swinging group." Everyone wants to go to Austin to be part of the Austin scene, including me. Which means, of course, that Austin is being crushed into something quite different than it's been. We don't know what that will be yet.

Dallas is the try-too-hard, don't-get-no-respect city. "The most un-Texas thing about Dallas is that it's self-conscious," Molly Ivins wrote. "Dallas is almost entirely middle class and worries obsessively about what other people think." When Boeing Corporation chose not to relocate in Dallas, the city was crushed as if it had been turned down for the prom. Dallas pleads with the world to acknowledge it as an "international city," but no one seems to be buying it. At one point in the eighties, lampposts of downtown Dallas were festooned with banners reading: "Dallas salutes the world." The world did not appear to notice.

Still, Dallas sits fat and happy as the epicenter of conspicuous consumption. Dallasites can think of no better way to spend a weekend than dressing up and going to the mall. Dallas likes big, expensive, and lots of it. "In Dallas, they all have big, big rings and big, big cars," observes my nine-year-old friend Ginny, a lifelong Dallasite.

Dallas has no real reason to be and grew on the prairie because some wheeling and dealing brought the railroad through town. Dallas is all business, no romance. J.R. and that whole well-funded crew live on in the soul of the city which, writes Ivins, "is located at the Tomb of the Unknown Shopper, a monument that has not yet been built, but it will be as soon as Dallas acquires a municipal sense of humor." (In fact, Dallas did build a big, expensive monument of a cattle drive, which has little to do with Dallas history and was humorless in a humorous way. A giant boardroom table would have been more appropriate, said one Dallas wag, when plans for the monument were being heatedly debated around town. And while we've all grown quite fond of the cattle drive, I still think wistfully of how much more fun a giant boardroom table would be.)

Other Texas cities make fun of Dallas and accuse it of pretentiousness and soullessness. These accusations are not lacking merit. Dallasites are often of two minds about it themselves, veering between boosterism and shame. "It's a nice place to live, but I wouldn't want to visit," is how one friend describes it. However, Dallas is located roughly equidistant from the coasts, and we have an international airport the size of Manhattan. Those are both pluses. Dallas has a lot of jobs. That's a plus. Housing is easy to find in Dallas, though in the spirit of "more is more" those houses are getting ridiculously large and commensurately expensive.

Dallas has great restaurants, one of the world's greatest skylines, decent though not spectacular museums, and it's big enough to attract big road shows. But when I have out-of-town guests, I always take them to Fort Worth.

Smaller Fort Worth, thirty miles to the west, maintains greater dignity than Dallas, with its genuine Western roots and a knack for cultural endeavors that work, including an elegant museum district; flourishing symphony, ballet, and opera; and the revitalized Sundance Square district, in downtown Fort Worth. Downtown Fort Worth is busy after dark while at 5 p.m. every evening, downtown Dallas empties out like school in July as everyone hightails it back to Plano, McKinney, and other towns in the city's northward sprawl. This is slowly changing—but very slowly.

The College Scene

"My gosh, you've been in Texas long enough to know the difference," said a friend in disgust recently, when I'd mixed up the nicknames for a couple of Texas universities.

Apparently not. I now know, however, having faced yet again a Texan's scorn, that UT is University of Texas, which is in Austin, and UTA is the University of Texas at Arlington. Live and learn.

Here's a rundown of some of the major Texas schools. Don't make any rash decisions from this, just factor it in. We're speaking strictly good times potential here. Weighing academic factors is not my job.

University of Texas: Located in Austin, this massive school of nearly 50,000 students is trying hard to change its rep as a party school, but that's hard to do in the good-time atmosphere of Austin. UT is so popular it recently had to close admissions to new students for a while. Among the nine other campuses in the University of Texas system are schools in Arlington (second largest campus); Dallas (no football team, but a championship chess team); El Paso (largest university in the U.S. with a majority Mexican-American student body); and San Antonio (the state's fastest growing public university).

UT alumni include Bill Moyers (highbrow journalist), Walter Cronkite (beloved news hound), Lady Bird Johnson (first lady and wildflower advocate), and Farrah Fawcett (babe-a-licious Hollywood star).

Texas A&M: Based in College Station and Texas's first public institute of higher education, A&M (originally the Agricultural & Mechanical College of Texas) has rabidly loyal students and alumni (known as former students), called Aggies. "Aggie" jokes are the Polish jokes of Texas, a leftover from the days when Aggie boys were farm boys without much l'arnin'. A&M has a complicated set of traditions, including the 12th Man football tradition; the now tragedy-tinged bonfire; and "Howdy Camp," a weekend-long orientation for new students in which, "We offer insight into the world that is Texas A&M, a few days to kick back and enjoy life before the semester begins, and above all the friendship that only Aggies understand!" The A&M Corps of Cadets is known as "the Founder of traditions and the keeper of the spirit." Don't mess with Aggies. Singer-songwriters Lyle Lovett and Robert Earl Keen together wrote "This Old Porch," which both have recorded, while students here.

Southern Methodist University: A private liberal arts school with a particularly good performing arts program, a high percentage of blonde students driving expensive cars, and a pretty campus on the edge of tony Highland Park. SMU churns out grads who make lots of money and donate it back. Alumni include Laura Bush (ladylike first lady), Beth Henley (Southern-fried playwright), and Aaron Spelling (television producer/mogul).

University of North Texas: An arty school in Denton, a groovy little college town thirty-five miles north of D/FW, UNT is the fourth largest university in Texas. UNT (formerly North Texas State University, formerly North Texas State College, formerly North Texas State Teachers College, formerly North Texas State Normal College, formerly North Texas Normal

College, formerly Texas Normal College and Teacher Training Institute) is particularly known for its highly competitive and well-respected jazz program, which offered the world's first degree in jazz. Alumni include Herb Ellis (jazz guitar legend) and Mean Joe Green (football player and Coca Cola commercial star), who got his nickname from the school's team, the Mean Greens.

Rice University: With just 4,200 students—undergrad and grad—Rice, in Houston, could practically fit into a UT restroom. Though once focused on the sciences, Rice now has respected programs in such interesting esoterica as Victorian literature and critical anthropology. It hardly seems Texan. Alumni include Larry McMurtry (Texas chronicler) and John Graves (modern-day Thoreau).

Baylor University: The world's largest Baptist university, Baylor officially took the "no dancing" rule off the books in 1996. Baylor is in poor old Waco, a God-fearin' city on the prairie forever burned into the world consciousness as the location of the David Koresh fiasco. The city had just sunk a bunch of money in museums and attractions and now all anybody wants to see is the empty field where the Koresh compound once stood. While the "Methodist" in SMU is just a suggestion, Baylor puts more emphasis on keeping the Christ in Baptist. Ann Richards and Olympian Michael Johnson are alumni, and President George W. was grand marshal of the school's homecoming parade, back in his governor days. ❧

Fort Worth hangs on to its honestly won cowtown image. Fort Worth was a stop on the old Chisholm Trail and has a beautifully restored Stockyards perfect for entertaining Yankee visitors who expect to see something Western. Fort Worth eschews Dallas' razzle-dazzle and maintains a slower pace than Dallas, Austin, or Houston.

Houston is Texas's biggest city and therefore "...falls naturally into the category of things to be taken seriously," McMurtry wrote. Houston has a cocktail in one hand and worldly wisdom in its twang. It's the wise gran dam of Texas cities. No matter how much other Texas cities grow, Houston will always be more grown up, with a sophisticated arts scene and municipal self-confidence that makes Dallas look needy and Austin look like a frat boy.

Houston is arty, with both alternative and mainstream arts, from the elegant Menil Collection to the Beer Can House and the annual Art Car show. The Houston Grand Opera is unafraid of challenging work, such as the world premier of "Nixon in China" in 1987, and is even given credibility—in the form of reviews—from *The New York Times, The Wall Street Journal,* and other such far-flung Yankee publications. ("Houston likes challenging art so long as it is well dressed," wrote a reviewer in London's *Financial Times*.) Even more than Dallas, Houston loves high society, loves to put on fancy clothes and smile for the society pages. Houston is the "wannabe city" says Pat, who moved there from Massachusetts seven years ago. "We've got the socialites like Diane Farb who attend every 'disease gala' and fund-raising activity that requires a ball gown. Then there is the gay and lesbian population in Montrose, and the dot-commers, a huge Asian population, who are in their twenties, drive Porsches, Beemers, Jags, and go clubbing downtown. Then there's the 'native born' Houstonians who participate in the Rodeo and every cookoff known to man."

While Houston strives, Dallas consumes conspicuously, and Austin rocks, San Antonio is very busy remembering the Alamo. San Antonio is proudly owned by all Texans. "It is Texas, and yet it transcends Texas in some way, as San Francisco transcends California, as New Orleans transcends Louisiana," McMurtry wrote. Home to the Institute of Texan Cultures, San Antonio is the most comfortably culturally diverse city in Texas, particularly in the mingling of Hispanics and Anglos. While the city does segregate itself, as much of Texas does (why do rich folk always drift north?), its cultural spice makes Yankee chicks feel comfy. "The other day I went out to lunch with a bunch of my friends from the newspaper,'" says Anne, a reporter in San Antonio. "There were eight people at the table, and I was the only one who was white. It was great."

San Antonio also is the crown jewel of Texas tourism. In the 1940s, the city turned a drainage ditch of a river into the Riverwalk, a collection of hotels, restaurants, and shops built along the San Antonio River. Now the Alamo and Riverwalk are the state's top tourist attraction, although visitors are invariably surprised to see that what remains of the Alamo is just a small building in the middle of downtown.

San Antonio tourism is frenetic, but the pace of the city is slow. "Sometimes I think it's not going anywhere, if you know what I mean" says Karen, who moved from Ohio a year ago. The responsibility of being home to the Alamo weighs heavily on San Antonio, and the city's commitment to its history is so great, the town can seem paused in time. There's not a lot to do in San Antonio once you've hit the tourist highlights. Theater is not big and the music tours that come to San Antonio are usually "fogey metal," sighs Anne. To keep busy you might go to Spurs (basketball) games, eat at little Tex-Mex dives, go to fiestas and festivals, hang out at clubs in Alamo Heights, or drive an hour to Austin where the real action is.

West Texas oil towns Midland and Odessa are money towns in the desert. Odessa made it into the national consciousness when H.G. Bissinger published *Friday Night Lights*, his Yankee's-eye view of Texas high school football, which focused on the Permian Panthers, and over which locals still hold a grudge. Midland has hit the map with homeboy George W. Bush, who came to town to try his hand at being an oil mogul. This part of Texas is the land of oil. It ain't purty, and it's not prosperous as it once was—the landscape is littered with rusting hulks of abandoned equipment—but West Texas has a powerful mystique. It's a great place to visit.

I've met a couple of the legends of West Texas: Barton Warnock, a botanist who identified thousands of West Texas wildflowers and loved the harsh land with a fierce and gentle passion; and Hallie Stillwell, who came to West Texas in a covered wagon and after a colorful frontier life, died a couple of months before her 100th birthday (see "I Am Woman Hear Me Jangle," page 163). In West Texas, as in nowhere else in the state, one still gets a whiff of everything Texas was before it was tamed.

I also remember driving through the vast scenery with Dadie Stillwell, Hallie's daughter, when she mildly pointed out the Stillwell Mountains, named for her father. "Why were they named for him?" I asked, expecting a colorful story of frontier settlement. "He bought them," Dadie replied, without a hint of irony. West Texas is practical and straightforward.

Corpus Christi has a sparkling bay, beaches, and a lot of retirees. It is quiet, clean, and low-key and nurtures an outdoors life of fishing and sailing. All I know of Port Arthur is that Janis Joplin was born there, which gives it Brownie points. I had a friend from Port Arthur, but he merely winced and shuddered delicately anytime I asked him what it was like. "For the other cities—Waco, Beaumont, the oil towns of East Texas (Lufkin, Longview, Tyler, Texarkana) and the triplets of the plains (Amarillo, Lubbock, Wichita Falls) generosity asks a kind silence," McMurtry wrote. But Molly Ivins claims Lubbock as her favorite Texas city. "Lubbock's a place that'll keep you honest," she wrote. "It's hard to be pretentious or affected if you're from Lubbock."

El Paso straddles cultures like San Antonio but with no tourist gloss. I spent a couple of days in El Paso once and liked it very much, even though there's not a lot of there there. El Paso's downtown seems paused some time in the 1940s, you're surrounded by desert, and you can walk through a turnstile to Mexico.

Once you have ascertained the city you will live in, you have to choose the right neighborhood. My first home in Dallas was a small house, the first time I'd ever lived in a single-family home. We had a lawn, and our neighbors kept roosters. I thought I was living in the country, and it was months before I understood my home was actually a pretty seamy corner of an urban neighborhood, a block from motels that rented by the hour. When I got the picture, I found a new place to live.

If you still have time to shop around for your neighborhood, take it. If you're moving to one of the large or mid-size cities, you will be able to find a neighborhood that is comfortable for you. Here is what you might not know yet about Texas: It has a lot more diversity than it lets on. I once saw a drag queen eating lunch in a bayside seafood restaurant in Corpus Christi. See what I'm getting at? We have everything all here, maybe not as much and you might need to look harder to find it, but it's there. And in some cases, we have more than you imagine. A little waltz through the 2000 census reveals that gay couples live in all but three Texas counties; Hispanics make up 32 percent of the population and are driving growth in the state overall (Bexar County, where San Antonio is located, is more than half Hispanic); Asians are at almost 3 percent (in parts of Houston, 11 percent); African-Americans are 11.5 percent; and more than 11 percent of people checked "other." It's nice to know there's a lot of "other" out there. (Incidentally, 71 percent of Texans were born in Texas, which means that 29 percent came from elsewhere. A lot of that would be Mexico, but we're part of that, too, as migration to the Southwest from other parts of the country is a national trend.)

Texans do seem to segregate themselves, and while some neighborhoods seem shockingly monocultural, the cities have plenty of ethnically diverse neighborhoods if you look for them. Or, you can find areas where everyone looks just like you, if that's what you want. Take your time choosing where to live and assimilation will be easier.

Everything Looks Better with a Panhandle: The Shape of Texas

By now you have noticed that there is no product that can't be improved by making it in the shape of Texas. If it isn't made in the shape of Texas, it has the shape of Texas on it, somewhere. Texas is ubiquitous in Texas. This is one way Texans show their Texas-pride.

Texas is a cool shape. Vaguely star-shaped, oddly symmetrical—with dusty West Texas balancing the torpid east—and instantly recognizable, the shape begs to be exploited and Texans make the most of it. Over time, the shape has become a visual shorthand for the Texas history and mythology. Can you look at the shape of Texas, even if it's just a praline, a change purse, or an egg salad sandwich, and not hear thundering cattle and cowboys' whoops? I hear LBJ too. And accordions. Willie Nelson. Ann Richards. I bet even people who have never been to Texas hear these things, or some version of them. Yet you could show me a matzo baked in the shape of New York State and I probably wouldn't even recognize it.

Of course Texas worship is not limited to its capabilities as a decorative motif. The feeling Texans have about Texas is passionate to the point of blindness. I say that with affection because there is something wonderful about Texans' staunch loyalty to their state. It's pointless to argue with a Texan about Texas, and in these parts it's considered exceedingly rude. Texas exists on two planes. There is the real Texas, in whose traffic jams you sit, and there is the iconic Texas, the platonic Texas, the Texas that makes Texans go all teary and run out and make hamburger dills in the shape of Texas. This is the Texas you leave the hell alone.

Texans fought hard for their state. (And remember, *real* Texans have been in the state for generations, so Texas history winds back into their own family histories.) Six flags have flown over Texas, which is a fact every schoolchild knows and you should too because it pleases the natives. The flags represent (in order): Spain, France, Mexico, Republic of Texas, Confederacy, the United States. Texas has a pledge of allegiance to the state flag that people actually recite at events such as city council meetings, and while most other states fly their flag lower than the U.S. flag, Texas flag regulations put the Texas flag at the same height as our nation's banner.

Texans' love-it-or-leave it attitude can be exasperating when it's used to resist any change, bad or good. But how nice it must be to feel so certain about your home. The way past, present, and future are cherished in Texas can be a beautiful thing. "I've seen it with football teams, with schools," says Anne from the East Coast with awe. "But never a *whole* state."

Chapter Three

Hot and Other Weather

"*You have two seasons here, right?*"

—*Tara, New Jersey, two years in Texas*

Chapter Three

*H*ow do you know when summer arrives in Texas? For me, it's the buzz of the first cicada. One minute it is not there, and then it is—or did I just not notice it before?

A dramatic change of seasons is one thing many Yankee chicks in Texas miss, but if you stay here long enough, you will become sensitive to the arrival of a new season.

Summer, the dominant season, is easy enough to recognize. It's hot, fire ants and mosquitoes take over the yard, cockroaches the size of spaniels emerge from wherever they winter (they call them "palmetto bugs" here—a ludicrously pretty name), and the racket of cicadas all but drowns out the hum of air conditioners. Nature's green seems exhausted, the plump foliage of spring is withered and dusty. With the sun blazing until 9 p.m., days seem impossibly long in summer. Summer Sundays seem a week long at least, especially if you do with them what you should, which is mix up a pitcher of something cold and delicious and remain motionless in the shade for as many hours as the ice holds up. Swimming pools are nice in summertime, although they get warm as bath water and are more psychologically refreshing than physically. If you don't have a swimming pool, wading pools are acceptable. I once had one just big enough to float a raft in, which I did, for many hours, spinning lazily, like a roulette wheel.

It doesn't rain much in summer. Really. "When they said it didn't rain in the summertime, I had no conception of that," says Karen. "When it does rain, everybody rejoices. In Ohio, they complained that it was a crappy day." But Texas summer rains are peculiar to Yankees who expect the shower to "break the heat." You step out your door after a summer downpour, expecting a fresh, washed breeze and instead get a face full of hot, moist air, like a wet washcloth.

If at 6 a.m. Saturday your neighborhood suddenly sounds as if it's being buzzed by the Japanese air force, that means it's summer and everyone is powering up lawnmowers, chain saws, and blowers to get the yard work done before the heat kicks in. But even these ambitions ebb as the heat settles in for the long haul. By August yard work is not much more than sprinklers and mowing if it's not a particularly bad summer, when lawns are burned brown despite good intentions. In bad summers, when watering may be restricted anyway as reservoirs get low, a lot of people just give up and let the lawn and garden go brown. The smartest gardeners plant native, heat resistant plants, which still might go brown in summer but then you can tell people you're simply working with nature rather than ignoring your landscaping. I use tough love in my landscape. If it can't take the heat and insists on water more than once a week, then so sad, bye-bye.

You are, by the way, allowed to complain about the heat in Texas. Everybody does. It's actually a form of bragging. The heat is always an acceptable topic of conversation, no matter how unnecessary the discussion might seem. "I mean, *duh*, It's Texas, it's July, what do you expect?" says Anne. "My favorite is when you come in, all dripping with sweat and feeling gross and melty, and some chipper someone who's been ensconced in the A/C all day says, 'Hot today, huh?' No, I just sweat for the hell of it."

Talking about the heat is similar to sweating, actually. It's venting.

Nothing wears out its welcome like Texas summer in September. We give it until about Halloween, and then we declare it over. October weather in Texas would qualify as summer anywhere else in the country, but by then we've simply had enough. In October women pull out their Halloween sweaters and matching socks. Trees turn color in one dramatic week. You have to be paying attention, but it happens.

Whenever summer doesn't transition directly into winter, as it is often does, fall is a delicious time in Texas. The air sometimes bears a resemblance to crisp, and you are sprung free of air-conditioned interiors to revel in the outdoors again. You can wear cotton sweaters with your shorts. It's State Fair time in Dallas—caramel apples and prize billy goats and the like. If you live in South Texas, you start looking for the fall migration of the Snowbirds—the winter Texans, midwesterners and northerners smart enough to realize that January in Corpus Christi beats the hell out of January in Minneapolis. Autumn may be just a brief interval and requires a finely tuned perception, but contrary to rumor, there is an autumn of sorts in Texas.

Winter gets rough in some parts of the state—Amarillo has some dastardly cold weather and in North and Central Texas, blue northers blow in straight across the plains, darkening the sky and sending the thermometer plummeting from balmy to bitter in minutes. If you hold your hand against a windowpane, you can feel the temperature drop as a blue norther rolls in. Blue northers blow in, hang around a day or two, then roll out. And then the sun shines again and Texas is magnificent.

Texas in spring is a giddy infatuation. Texas in winter is an abiding love. Dazzling 70-degree days can hit without warning at any time, even the middle of January. In some parts of Texas, icy roads are a non-issue. Trees might be bare but the sky is

Things to know about Texas weather

- On the weather report, a "watch" means meteorologists are monitoring areas of potential storm development. A "warning" means a dangerous storm has been spotted and confirmed. A warning is more serious than a watch.
- In summer, weather forecasters will daily mention a 20 percent chance of rain. That's the "never-say-never" statistic. Ignore it. It won't rain.
- If you actually hear a tornado siren, get away from windows and into your designated interior safe room. If you're in your car and see a tornado, get out of the car and go into a sturdy building or lie flat in a ditch or low-lying area. But first videotape the twister because TV news loves that kind of footage.
- Don't be silly about the heat. Sunscreen, lots of water—you know what to do. Do it.
- April showers bring spring allergies. The molds and pollens of Texas are a beast for the allergic. Plan accordingly.
- If you exercise outside, do it in the morning whenever possible in summertime. Evenings may be cooler back home, but down here when the sidewalk has been baking in the sun and the day's pollution is hanging in the air, evenings are only when you have no other choice. I get hot and bothered when I spot businessmen near their hotels—clearly out-of-towners—trying to fit in their day's run at lunchtime. What are they, crazy? ❧

usually sapphire, cold snaps come and go, and sometimes you don't even need a jacket. That's winter. It's a beautiful thing.

Most of Texas gets little or no snow, but it does make an occasional appearance in the northern parts of the state. Little is so tragic to the Yankee chick as the withered little excuses for snowmen children build on those rare occasions when we have enough snow in Dallas for such attempts. Texas snowmen are about two-feet tall and leprous looking, made as much with mud and dead leaves as snow.

But I can sacrifice a few snowmen for thousands of sparkling Texas winter days. Texas winters have kept me in the state for twenty years. The sunshine of Texas is nourishment and too long a stretch without it oppresses the spirit. When I am homesick for New York, I remind myself of waiting for a bus home after work on dank, cold, January evenings, with slush around my ankles and too damn many people pushing around me. I remember looking for a taxi at 3 a.m. on 86th Street and Lexington, with an icy wind whipping off the East River, slicing through my coat and clothes and making my eyes water. (Not to mention the 4-inch heels, which were killing me.) I remember February. And I wrote that sentence even before opening Florence King's *Southern Ladies and Gentleman* and reading her experience as a southerner in the north. "Nothing is more likely to start me screaming like a madwoman than New York in February with its piles of blackened snow full of yellow holes drilled by dogs," she wrote. That's where that Southerner and this Yankee agree. Glorious winter days in Texas make up for those last two "when is it going to end?" months of summer. So does spring.

Even the newly transplanted can recognize spring, the most magnificent season of all in Texas. Spring is fragrant and gentle, raging and tumultuous. Spring is carpets of wildflowers and storms the likes of which few Yankee chicks have ever witnessed. When Ellen first moved to Texas from New York, she and her daughter stepped out of a supermarket as a lightning storm rolled in. They stood transfixed by the dramatic show. "People who passed also looked up, trying to figure out what we were looking at," Ellen says. "Finally, somebody said, 'Just moved here, huh?'"

In the Robert Altman movie *Dr. T. and the Women,* which takes place in Dallas, the story blows in on one spectacular storm and blows out on another. The storms of spring are high drama, an epic introduction to the Great Beast Summer. They come crashing through in the middle of the night, sending you bolt upright in bed. Lightning is like the zig-zags of comic strips, walls of rain fall, then solidify into what is familiarly known as "golf-ball-sized hail." Roofers and auto-body shops do good business in spring, and hail-damaged cars sell cheap. You spend a lot of time resetting all your digital clocks during storm season. I love a good storm, and my husband and I will stand on the porch to feel the electric wind and rushing rain for as long as it feels safe. Texas storms are Mother Nature's libido.

However, I have learned to respect them. I didn't take the whole storm business seriously when I first arrived. But after watching the sky turn green, hearing lightning strike a tree, and seeing the aftermath of a flash flood, I've come to understand that this is no-fooling weather. The hurricane that hit Galveston in 1900 remains the deadliest natural disaster in the history of the United States; over 6,000 people lost their lives and more than 3,600 buildings were destroyed in one storm.

Texans keep an eye on the weather and plan accordingly. In Houston, which gets rained underwater sometimes and where storm season is anytime, free storm-tracking maps in Spanish and English are distributed through convenience stores and newspapers so residents can follow storms as meteorologists track them. Anywhere you live, a tornado siren is something to take seriously. When we hear it, Tom and I take the ladder, vacuum, and TV trays out of a hall closet, round up the pets, and stand ready to take shelter. And most important, we turn on the TV to check in with our favorite meteorologists.

Texas meteorologists are celebrities, and they owe their stature to spring. During much of the year, weathermen are reduced to parroting "Sunny and hot," every night, with digressions into the pollen count. But in the spring, meteorologists get to interrupt regular programming, stand in front of dire-looking maps with red zones of danger, talk weatherspeak, and gravely advise the public to "take cover." Texas meteorologists must be solemn and reassuring but with a sense of humor, since predicting weather in Texas is a fool's job. "If you don't like the weather in Texas," the saying goes, "just wait a minute. It will change."

And of course with April showers, blah, blah, blah, Texas wildflowers. Texas wildflowers are a state treasure. "I am convinced that God did Texas wildflowers last, because when he finished, there was no way to top it," says Ginnie from Ohio.

Texans watch the progress of wildflowers like New Englanders watch leaves, trying to time their weekend getaways to the exact moment the flowers are at their peak. On those weekends, fields of wildflowers are littered with babies in Sunday finery and their parents crouching nearby with cameras. Lady Bird Johnson is commonly credited for the stunning displays of flowers along Texas highways, although she didn't actually go out like Johnny Bluebonnetseed and plant them.

Rather, she promoted the Highway Beautification Act of 1965 and founded the National Wildflower Research Center, now renamed for her, in the Hill Country. The bluebonnet beat out the prickly pear cactus bloom and the cotton boll to be named the state flower of Texas back in 1901, thanks to the efforts of the National Society of the Colonial Dames of America in the State of Texas. (Who could argue with a group bearing that name?) You might hear that picking bluebonnets is illegal, but this is a myth. Picking anything in state and national parks is illegal all over the country, but picking wildflowers in Texas, even bluebonnets, by the roadsides will not put you in the hoosegow. So go, enjoy the brief, colorful interval before summer kicks in and everything turns brown again.

All this weather takes place against a background of the Texas sky for which I have only the most awed appreciation. Having spent the first twenty-two years of my life seeing only fragments of sky between buildings, nothing prepared me for the sheer expanse of Texas sky. Texas sunsets are kinetic art, its sunrises a morning caress. Watching a storm move across the sky, blotting out blue with gray, is better than TV. The Texas sky is epic. Watch the sky and you see time, space, and the seasons.

Nature's Other Seasons

Post-Drought Disgusting Crickets Season: Drought followed by rain can produce a crop of crickets that will give a Yankee chick nightmares. There are piles of them in parking lots, they lurk in hallways, they die in the walls. Did you know dead crickets can kick up a stench? Yup.

Red Devil Season: After the spring rains, when the ground is softened, the fire ant mounds start popping up. Fire ants are very small, but their bites hurt like hell. Take no prisoners. My garden is organic, except for fire ants. I use evil-smelling chemicals on those. Be sure to read the directions for use. My husband and I just poured ant bait on mounds for years, before someone explained that we needed to sprinkle it around the mound, not in it. Oh.

Rampant Robin Season: Back East, the first robin of spring is a transcendental moment, a fleeting and promising portent of the changing season. Down here, I look out my window one day in spring and the lawn is solid robins, terrorizing every worm on the property.

Texas is on a major "flyway," and when the birds come through, it's in quantity. The robin thing spooked me the first time I saw it, but now I pretend to dabble in birdwatching. I have binoculars and a bird book, although the only bird I've ever correctly identified myself is the cedar waxwing, which is kind of like identifying a pigeon in New York.

Excessive Grackle Season: In winter, great flocks of grackles—a black bird with a piercing vibrato warble—roost in Texas city trees, making a racket and rendering the sidewalk beneath them unusable. City crews have tried everything from loud music to tree hair nets to plastic owls. Apparently the running joke among city employees about the fake owls is that you have to take them down when they get so covered with bird poop, you can't tell they're owls anymore.

Nasty Water Season: Mid-summer, when the reservoirs are cooked to a turn, North Texas water gets a bloom of algae that makes the tap water taste like it spent the winter fermenting in a rusting tub. You'll want bottled water for everything, including coffee.

Creature from the Black Lagoon Season: When it's warm and very rainy, palmetto bugs (giant roaches) like to come in out of the wet and into your nice, dry home. Just know that everyone has them sometimes; it says nothing about your housekeeping habits. "Have I gotten used to them after twenty-eight years?" asks Barbara from Oregon. "No, I just learned a higher level of tolerance. Now the tiny reptiles that inhabit my house in the summer, slithering under my bare feet and keeping these other bugs under control, I see as a huge plus. They become part of the family and I miss them when the weather cools."

Chapter Four

Texas Cuisine

"My mother's chili has Campbell's tomato soup in it."

—Pam, New York, thirty years in Texas

*T*exas specialties are not healthy, low-cal, or chic. They're greasy and cheesy and spicy and fatty and all the other nutritional dwarves. They're also addictive. Texas's Big Four—Tex-Mex, chili, barbecue, and home cooking—each are contributions by one of the state's cultures. Mexican cooking is the basis for Tex-Mex, of course, and it also influenced chili, although Texas-style chili is generally regarded as being invented in San Antonio. Texas barbecue was nurtured along by Germans and Czechs, who know what to do with a wurst. Home cooking and soul food are sisters, with little different but the name and the neighborhood.

To some extent Texas foods are an acquired taste. The Elmer's Glue called white gravy might send you running from the table the first time it's put in front of you, but before long you'll crave it on everything that doesn't already have chili con carne on it. Chicken-fried steak might seem suspiciously like batter fried shoe leather the first time someone talks you into trying it, but stick around long enough and you'll find yourself ordering it on those occasions when you feel like you deserve a special treat. You'll need initiation into the mysteries of the full Tex-Mex menu, especially if you live in San Antonio or near the border, where they're dead serious about Mexican food. "Up north it's fajitas, tacos, burritos," says Karen. "Down here they've got all these crazy things, I don't know what the heck they are. I have to ask."

When I first moved down, my system could tolerate Mexican food only about once a month. These days the first thing I do when I've been traveling (sometimes not even stopping home to drop off my luggage first) is satisfy my Mexican food craving. A week is far too long to go without Mexican food. Two weeks and I'm hurting. Mexican food can be great in fancy places but it's often better in dives, and everyone has their favorites. Anytime anyone says, "I found a great new Mexican place..." check it out. The depth of great Mexican places in Texas is untapped.

Forgetting all health concerns in a Mexican restaurant is surprisingly easy. If you feel like indulging a false sense of virtue, chicken fajitas are not too bad; corn tortillas are less fattening than flour; soft tacos (mop off some grease with your napkins) might not kill you as fast as crispy. Mexican restaurants often do good things with fish. I love ceviche, which is raw fish "cooked" in lime juice, but I need to feel very confident of the restaurant before I'll order it. If you find grilled catfish on a Mexican menu, it's often good. Chile relleno, a pepper filled with meat, battered, and fried, is for when you're throwing calories to the wind. It's the Big Mac of Mexican food. Of course, it's all moot by the time you've thrown down your first basket of chips. "Don't forget, they call it Fat Antonio," says Karen. "Everyone eats, like, twenty tortillas a day here."

Oh, and speaking of Mexican foods that you don't know what the heck they are, you should know that menudo is tripe soup. It's supposed to be good for a hangover, possibly by causing you to hurl all the offending substances you poured into your body the night before. Tripe looks exactly like pig stomach, which it is, of course. Like Rocky Mountain oysters, menudo is a delicacy to many people, but you should know what you're getting into. Otherwise, you really can't go too wrong in a Mexican restaurant when you venture off the enchilada trail.

Equally unhealthy and delicious is home cooking, with its ruling entree, chicken-fried steak. Larry McMurtry has said, "only a rank degenerate would drive 1,500 miles across Texas without eating a chicken-fried steak." Of course you know, chicken-fried steak is not chicken and it's only marginally steak. It is a low-rent hunk of tenderized round that is fried like one would fry chicken (which appears on menus as "chicken-fried chicken." Go figure). Chicken-fried steak goes best with mashed potatoes, and both must be slathered in white gravy. Sometimes I'll meet a friend for lunch and we'll both order chicken-fried steak and apologize to each other the entire time we're eating it. "I just had a craving for chicken-fried steak," we'll confess, again and again, while we sop up cream gravy with our deep-fried meat.

Chicken-fried steak is often the centerpiece of a traditional "meat and three" meal, standard at, though not exclusive to, cafeteria-style restaurants. Meat and three is a meat and three vegetables, although it's not as healthy as it sounds since the vegetable are usually cooked in bacon fat to the consistency of tapioca, or breaded and fried, which is practically the only palatable way to eat okra. (I admit that since I've been south awhile, I have an easier time with boiled okra, despite its unfortunate snot-like consistency.) Greens (turnip, mustard) are a home cooking and soul food staple and they're full of vitamins, but unless cooked by a magician, they're tastiest when cooked with a hunk of fatty pork. You don't find chitterlings in many home-cooking restaurants, but they do turn up in soul food restaurants. I ordered chitterlings (pronounced "chitlins") once. All I can say is: intestines. If you like that kind of thing, have at it.

Home-cooking salads are a bowl of iceberg lettuce and carrot shreds drenched in ranch dressing, another diet staple here. "I eat ranch dressing on everything," says Maggie from

St. Louis, with heartfelt appreciation. To add to the bounty of delicious fatty foods, you also get rolls and cornbread with your meat and three. It is all properly washed down with iced tea, which is served to you in gallon jugs with handles. If you order tea in Texas, you get iced tea. If you want it hot, say so. In soul food restaurants and some small-town joints, iced tea may be served sweetened. Very sweetened. Be sure to ask. Waiters rarely let your iced tea glass empty more than halfway. Laura from Iowa reports that her Fort Worth beau scales waiters' tips according to how fast they refill the iced tea glass. And once on a visit to New York, I paid $1.50 for a dainty little glass of iced tea at Tavern on the Green and then another $1.50 for the refill. I've never felt more like an indignant Texan than I did then. Coffee cups also are bottomless in Texas and on occasion I've had to throw myself bodily across mine to prevent the waitress from pouring that unnecessary 73rd cup.

Another meat and three staple, beans, are the bridge connecting the cuisines of Texas. Pinto beans and green beans are very home-cooking; ranch beans come with barbecue; frijoles turn up on every Tex-Mex platter, and pinto beans are allowed as a side dish to chili although some people (I'm not naming names) have been reputed to put kidney beans in chili, despite the adage that "If you know beans about chili you know chili has no beans." Ah, screw it—I put beans in my chili and the Chili Appreciation Society International has not yet exiled me to Cincinnati, where they put spaghetti in their chili, which I think we can all agree is disgusting. In *Fixin' to Party, Texas Style*, author Helen Bryant spews the no-beans party line, but then admits she and her Texan husband serve their chili over *rice*, so I think we're just splitting hairs here. But chiliheads are very strict so be cautious (see "Knowing Beans About It" page 53).

Like so many other things in Texas, food is a testy subject. "Three topics upon which southerners never agree are religion, politics, and barbecue," the *Encyclopedia of Southern Culture* cautions. Southerners in other states don't consider Texas barbecue worth discussing because it is beef instead of pork. Rambling around the web one day, I stumbled upon this statement on an extensive site about barbecue: "For the purposes of this paper, the one nondebatable component of barbecue is pork.... With apologies to the dedicated barbecue chefs of Owensboro and southwestern Texas, Kentucky's misbegotten notion of mutton and the beef and mesquite of Texas simply *do not qualify as barbecue ...* " (italics mine).

Well, that notwithstanding, Texas brisket is beef of the gods. You eat it sliced on a plate with beans and potato salad or coleslaw and an overachieving slice of toasted white bread known as Texas Toast. You can also get beef sandwiches, sliced or chopped, although my friend Texan John thinks chopped beef is a crime against nature and holds those who eat it in deepest contempt. Ribs are also a big item, pork and sometimes beef. Beef ribs are a little organic for my taste. They're bigger (naturally) and tougher, and you actually feel like you're gnawing on the rib of a cow. Pork ribs are more tender, and there's all that yummy charred fat.

Many a grand vacation has been spent driving around Central Texas and sampling the barbecue and sausages. My husband and I don't go to Austin without detouring to Elgin, home to the Southside Market and our favorite hot links. (We also have obligatory stops for kolaches and beef jerky.) Towns such as Lockhart, Elgin, Luling, Driftwood, all have beloved barbecue joints. At some places, your meat is slapped down in front of you on a piece of greasy brown paper, and at a couple, side dishes are considered a contemptible frill. At others, traditional sides are potato salad, which varies from place to place (sweet, savory, mayo-based, mustard-based), coleslaw, and pinto beans. Barbecue sauce also can be a touchy subject. My husband once asked for sauce at a place in Glen Rose. "Most people don't think it needs it," said the woman who served him, looking deeply wounded.

Many places cook only so much meat and no more, so if you arrive too late you're SOL. We've driven 90 minutes to our favorite place for ribs and arrived too late. No tragedy, though; the ribbus interruptus forced us to try the new place down the street, which we ended up liking even better.

Which leads us, conveniently, to the subject of deprivation. Texas has a lot of good eating, but it doesn't have everything Yankee chicks want. The good news is that many ethnic foods, particularly Asian, are increasingly common and of high quality both in restaurants and in groceries. Though the bigger cities have the most selection of Asian restaurants, these are reaching such saturation that spillover into smaller cities and towns is inevitable.

Everything else is hit or miss.

For example, good Italian food just isn't as easy to find as many Yanks are used to. "When I lived in Longview, the only Italian restaurant in town had a revolving bucket. It was spaghetti-to-go in a bucket," says Judy from New York. Rett, from New Jersey, says when her father came to visit Texas the first time, "he filled his suitcase with salami and provolone cheese, as if his daughter was starving." Rett continues her quest for a really good pizza but has just about given up on finding Italian sweet sausage that meets her standards.

Forget grabbing a quick slice of pizza for lunch, too. Texas is not really a "slice" kinda place. Here you get a whole pizza. If you're alone, you get an individual pizza. And when I once ordered a "pie" at a Dallas pizzeria, the guy behind the counter said with a happy grin, "New York." I asked how he knew. "Here they say, 'I'd like a *pizza*,'" he explained, and we shared a smile at the absurdity of the phrase.

Pizza is a sore point here. "In San Antonio, they voted Dominoes the best pizza place," says Anne. "'Nuff said." It's hard to describe how the pizza is different, but it is. Not enough sauce, maybe. Too much cheese. Bready crusts. It's just different and you either get used to it or you do without.

In Dallas, Houston, and Austin, you should be able to track down at least one deli for pastrami, corned beef, matzo balls and the like, though the meals probably won't be served with the delicious wise-guy attitude you get in Yankee Jewish delis. (And pizzerias, for that matter. When Judy moved from New York City to Longview and was "very pregnant and very homesick," she went to a mall one day. "I'm walking along and I hear, 'Whattyamean you don't likeada pizza.' And I see this very Italian, passionate guy is upset somebody had complained about the pizza. It was like a beacon. This poor young thing who'd complained, she didn't know what to do. So I just got in his face, *'Whattya givin' her a hard time for?'* It was the most liberating experience. We went back and forth. Hands were flying everywhere. He gave me free pizza. By the time we were done having an argument, I'd had lunch. I went back there whenever I got homesick.")

One Houston deli claims to have a little old Jewish lady who makes their chopped liver. And when the waiter puts a bowl of dills and half-sours in front of me at my favorite Dallas deli, I feel a twinge of home. But for the most part, you can't expect to be transported back to the old country at a Texas deli, either by food or ambience. They're too sunny and civilized and nobody is yelling. And I have yet to find a Jewish rye that can compare with the bread back home.

Fresh seafood is hard to come by and when you do, you pay. "There are no STEAMERS here," Pat from Massachusetts wails. "No little neck or long neck clams. When I first moved here, I thought there were *lots* of places that sold them. Then I found out that 'long necks' meant beer and not clams."

We do have shrimp from the bays of Texas, and plenty of fresh river food like catfish and crawfish in season (roughly February to mid-June), but that's about it. Although I can tear a Maine lobster apart with my bare hands, I haven't yet been drawn into the whole crawfish head-sucking cult, which is more a Louisiana passion than Texas. Otherwise, I eat sushi and catfish and salmon sometimes, but most of my seafood intake occurs when I travel.

You do your best. While you might be able to find Philly cheese steaks, meatball sandwiches, and Reubens, they may or may not be quite right. You grade on a curve, make your deals with the devil. I eat Pizza Hut pizzas with chicken and jalapeños. It's crazy, I know. Don't tell my old gang on the Lower East Side.

All-night diners are rare. When I reel out of a nightclub, ears ringing and feet aching, I still crave a Greek coffee shop breakfast, with plates of grease served up in a variety of tantalizing ways: home fries to English muffin. I'd even settle for Denny's, but the best I can find without going out of my way is an all-night Jack In The Box. I settle for a PB&J foldover eaten over the sink.

You can't get Sabrett's hot dogs down here, but you can get wicked good wursts all over Central Texas, so it's a fair trade —although I usually indulge myself with one good street vendor rats'-nostrils-and-cockroach dawg buried in sauerkraut when I visit New York. I also pack some bagels to take home (I'm told perfectly good bagels are available in Dallas but remain skeptical) and lox if I can afford it. I used to bring home boxes of Drake's Funnybones, which I kept in the freezer and rationed carefully. In recent years a local supermarket has started carrying Drake's Cakes (also Tastee Cakes from Philly, Linda is happy to report), but Funnybones are still a rare and wonderful occurrence.

I eat a lot on visits home, wolfing down all the foods I miss most. But these days, after about a week of Stromboli pizza, pirogi, sour dills, and cheap falafel, those cravings fade and the Tex-Mex heebie jeebies set in. And it's time to return to my other home.

Knowing Beans About It: Chili

Chili, which is commonly believed to have been invented in San Antonio, is the state dish of Texas and it's more than an icon, it's a cult. "Real chili con carne is a haunting, mystic thing," Frank X. Tolbert writes in *A Bowl of Red*, a compendium of chili lore from one of the dish's greatest proponents. He quotes Will Rogers as calling it "a bowl of blessedness." Chili has its own appreciation society, the Chili Appreciation Society International. And chiliheads are as strict as they are passionate. Tolbert tells of CASI founder George Haddaway hurling a bowl of chili at the chef of a Houston airport café for the sin of putting Boston baked beans in the chili, which is offensive to a Texan on many levels, palate included.

Dedicated chiliheads follow chili cookoffs all over the state, both to show off their recipes and to blow off steam in some of the wildest bacchanals this side of spring break. "I cooked at every cookoff every weekend in the state for eleven years and went to Terlingua every year. God, it was fun! Wild, insane, crazy, probably even dangerous, but *buckets* of fun," says Ginnie from Ohio, who has been in Texas forty-six years.

Terlingua is the big daddy of chili cookoffs. The oft-told tale of its roots is this: Frank X. Tolbert, a *Dallas Morning News* columnist, read a column by New York writer H. Allen Smith in which he claimed he made the best chili in the world. Coming from a

Yankee, these were fightin' words, so Tolbert arranged a cooking contest between Smith and Wick Fowler, another newspaper writer whose packaged chili seasoning mix is still a Texas kitchen staple. (See "B.Y.O.M." page 207.) According to Kirby Warnock, editor and publisher of *Big Bend Quarterly*, the contest was set in the remote West Texas ghost town of Terlingua because a friend of the writer, race driver Carroll Shelby (who also has his own packaged chili mix), had some land down there he wanted to sell and needed a publicity stunt to draw attention to it. Hundreds of people showed up for the contest and to camp out on the rugged desert terrain, despite the fact that Terlingua is 270 miles from the nearest commercial airport. "Aware of the PR value of the moment, the judges declared a tie, meaning that everyone had to come back and do it again next year," Warnock writes.

Everyone did, and did again, and again and the party kept growing until now thousands of people swarm to Terlingua each year for what now is actually two massive cookoffs over the same weekend. The Original International Frank X. Tolbert-Wick Fowler Memorial Championship Chili Cookoff and the Chili Appreciation Society International Cookoff are separate events as a result of some complicated dust-up among cookoff founders. I've read many accounts of the split between factions and still don't understand exactly what happened. It appears to be about rules and how many there should be, but people still bicker over who was wrong. The end result is two similar events that hate each other's guts.

Yankee chicks venturing here should prepare themselves for tawdry costumes, dirty jokes, wet T-shirt contests, and a good-naturedly low standard of behavior. That's what Terlingua is about, and it is the creme de la cookoff, although not the only one. Hundreds of other cookoffs throughout the state have varying levels of emphasis on chili v. beer, but all are guaranteed to be rollicking.

Chili cookoff chili is richer than what you might serve at home. It's made with good cuts of meat and no beans unless you want trouble. Chili cookoff competitors are protective of their recipes but have been known to put unlikely ingredients into their chili, including hair tonic and cigarette ashes "There's been some I wouldn't want to touch," a judge once confessed to me at the Hell Hath No Fury Ladies Sate Championship Cookoff in Luckenbach. However, warns Helen Bryant in *Fixin' to Party, Texas Style,* if you're judging the chili, "...any making of faces or whispering of 'yuck' draws a reprimand."

As a chili cookoff visitor, you might not actually get to eat a lot of chili. You walk around with a little cup and spoon and competitors dish out small tastes. When they get low on chili, they stop doling it out to save it for the judges.

The cult of the chili cookoff has elevated chili to extraordinary heights, but the dish itself is deserving. Little is more cheering on a winter afternoon than a bowl of red. Lots of people are happy to share chili recipes so ask around. If you're serving chili to

Texans, remember that chili with no kick is like pastrami with no mustard, so toughen up. Two-alarm chili is for sissies. "I went on a campaign to stop being a chili wimp," says Linda from Pennsylvania.

To bean or not to bean? I scoured *A Bowl of Red* and although Tolbert addresses the non-bean issue in passing, he never explains the prejudice. However, he does note that in chili's earliest days, the bowl didn't even contain tomatoes or onions. It was just meat, chile peppers, and spices. Things change. What you do behind closed doors is your own business, even if it involves beans and ground meat. Just don't serve it to a chilihead. ♥

Chapter Five

Courthouse Squares, Shriners, and You

"*We go to Athens for the Miss Black-Eyed Pea Contest. It's so small-town Texas, girls get up and sing 'God Bless America' and recite that Dear Abby thing, 'Dear God I'm Only Seventeen.' People outside Texas don't know these things are real.*"

—Melanie, Baltimore, eleven years in Texas

*O*nce you're settled in the right town, in the perfect neighborhood, in your dream house, get your Yankee butt out of town and explore the state.

The size of Texas, its weather extremes, its diversity of terrain, its sunsets, its wildflowers, its deserts, its mountains (yeah, mountains), even its highways are dramatic and compelling and among the reasons I remain in Texas. It should be written somewhere (and now I suppose it is) that within a year of moving here, Yankees should be required to pack a cooler, kick off their shoes, pop Hank Williams in the CD player, and take a road trip through as much of Texas as time allows. It's the only way to understand where you're living.

One of the best things about Texas is Texas. At 267,339 square miles, the state is guaranteed to contain something you will absolutely love, even if you're otherwise generally ambivalent about it. If you live in Texas and don't explore, you are not permitted to pass judgment on the state even among other Yankees because you don't know diddly.

Texans seeing Texas account for almost half the $10 billion tourists spend in the state annually. Texas is huge and has lots to see, and Texans are boastful about knowing their way around it. Everyone, native and not, has a favorite B&B, small-town festival, tubing river (involving an inner tube, a cooler, and a leisurely float), South Padre tradition, or all of the above. In all my years in New York, I never saw Albany or Buffalo or even White Plains, but I have been to El Paso, Midland, and Amarillo.

I have traveled the globe, and one of my favorite places on it is Big Bend National Park, which is among the most stirring, dramatic, and raw landscapes I've ever seen. This is the Texas of our national fantasy, with roadrunners skirting the road, tarantulas the size of teacups scuttling across it, javelinas (wild pigs) nosing around at twilight, and plainspoken, weathered folk descended from the hardy pioneers who settled the region.

Yankee Chicks' Texas Tour

After you've seen the sights of your town, here's some stuff worth traveling to.

Big Bend National Park: How often do I need to say this? It's spectacular. Book into the historic Gage Hotel in tiny Marathon, thirty miles from the park gate, or in the Chisos Mountains Lodge, a park facility in the piney "bowl" of the Chisos Mountains. Guided rafting trips are offered on the Rio Grande, including Texas music and gourmet trips. Be sure to visit the Hallie Stillwell Hall of Fame Museum for insight into the sort of sturdy pioneer stock that true Texas chicks come from. The Big Bend area is excellent for birding as well. Key advice for exploring the area: Never pass by a gas station or a bathroom without stopping to fill or empty.

The Hill Country: Central Texas's towns, hills, and rivers are like a Texas-sized amusement park for tourists, with eating (barbecue, see "Texas Cuisine" page 43); hiking (climb Enchanted Rock, for one); swimming (various companies can set you up for a day of tubing on the Guadalupe River); antiquing; and general goofin' around. You'll still hear German and Czech accents in some part of the state. And all Yanks should spend at least one weekend slackering around Austin to see why Texans love it so much. Everyone has their favorite Hill Country corners—poll the locals to plan your trip or just get in the car and explore. Spring is the best time, when the wildflowers are in bloom, but no time is a bad time for the Hill Country.

Galveston: I love the immigrant vibe of this once-prosperous port city, now a restored historical gem with a jaunty, eccentric tropical air. Galveston was targeted as a port of entry for Eastern European immigrants when New York's ghettos overcrowded, which explains the concentration of Texas towns with names like Gruene, New Braunfels, and Schulenberg. Galveston also has a collection of elaborate mansions that withstood the Great Storm of 1900, which wiped the island nearly flat. The Strand, named for London's financial district, is a collection of Victorian buildings on the National Register of Historic Places and the Seaport, now housing museums, shops, and restaurants.

Cadillac Ranch: You've seen the pictures, now see the real thing: ten Cadillacs planted nose first in a flat West Texas landscape. It's off Highway 40 in Amarillo and you can easily be the only person there, which makes the experience even more transcendent. The Ranch is the work of eccentric millionaire Stanley Marsh 3 and a collective of artists known as the Ant Farm. There's not a whole lot else to do in Amarillo besides visit Palo Duro Canyon and try to eat a 72-ounce steak at the Big Texan Steak House, the restaurant with the giant cow/obligatory Amarillo photo-op. Eat the entire steak and all the fixings and it's free. Amarillo is where Oprah was put on trial for allegedly defaming the beef industry.

Padre Island National Seashore: South Padre is fun for a funky resort vacation, but the national seashore—neglected and struggling—is affecting as only pure nature can be. The sweeping dunes and tidal flats of the national seashore, a protected sea turtles breeding ground and premier bird watching spot, is barely touched Texas, unless you count the tire tracks, since it's legal to drive on these beaches. Nonetheless, outdoorsy Yankee chicks should appreciate the sincerity of this natural spot.

Bandera: When out-of-town kids want a cowboy experience, take them to a dude ranch in Bandera, "The Cowboy Capital of the World" and home to a number of guest ranches, many of which took to welcoming dudes when the Depression took ranching down. The ranches' twice-daily horseback rides are nose-to-tail plods through glorious scenery, and the ambience is pure cowboy kitsch. Big, cholesterol-laden meals are served family-style in the lodges, and in the evenings grown-up guests go watch cowboy bands in town. You are almost guaranteed to hear tourists speaking German here. As a rule, the more cowboy the ambience, the more other languages you'll hear out of visitors. ❧

Texas is big. Yes, you know that, but until you've seen it, border to border, you don't know how big big is. Roads stretch straight into the horizon and then another horizon after that, and another after that. Driving a Texas highway in the afternoon sun is like flying. Sadly, the roads between the major cities are being swallowed by sprawl, but you can still find places where Texas looks like Texas. Head for the Panhandle, Big Bend, and parts of South Texas. Drive through the King Ranch.

Basic Texas geography is this: North Texas is the plains, widely considered a good place to make a living. Otherwise, it's mostly flat. Coming home to Dallas after visiting any place graced with natural beauty can make a Yankee chick question her sanity. Central Texas is the Hill Country, where all good Texans hope to go when they retire. This is the regions of weekend getaways, lazy rivers, barbecue, and wildflowers. East Texas is as much Louisiana as Texas: moist and Spanish moss-draped, more southern style than western. West Texas is the biggest part of big Texas. It's huge and it's harsh and haunting. My friend Kirby, whose West Texas roots go back generations, says, "Here we say that everything either bites, stings, sticks, or breaks your heart." West Texas is achingly beautiful, home to the golden Davis Mountains, the Chisos Mountains—which look a little like Colorado when you enter the basin—and the vast Chihuahuan Desert, which looks like the moon.

The Panhandle is another moonscape. I spent a weekend in Amarillo once to visit Palo Duro Canyon, which I've heard called "the Grand Canyon of Texas," with typical Texas hyperbole. It's a nice red rock canyon, but you could fit several of it into the Grand Canyon with room left over for the giant cow outside the Big Texan Steak House, Amarillo's other tourist attraction. The Panhandle is hardcore Texas and an acquired taste. I recently met an Amarillo native who longs to move home from Dallas. "In Amarillo, you can shake a person's hand and believe him," she said wistfully.

Yankee chicks accustomed to the dramatic shorelines of Maine or Northern California may be underwhelmed by the Texas coast, where the baked earth just sort of sighs and slips into the warm sea. And of course, there is that embarrassing problem of oil globs—among the toiletries in Galveston motels are tar-removal wipes for your feet after a day on the beach. South Padre beaches are wide and inviting (and to be avoided during the pubescent bacchanal of Spring Break), but I prefer the coast's more rustic beaches, with grasslands marching nearly up to the water and a sort of cozy, shabby fisherman air. South Texas also is one of the nation's best areas for bird watching because it's located on a major flyway. Pat from Massachusetts appreciates Houston's unpretentious year-round sailing. "It's very relaxed down here," she says. "I like it a lot better than back East, actually."

While Texans do love to boat and fish and drink beer while zipping around on annoying personal watercraft on the state's lakes, Yankee chicks are often taken aback by their first glimpse of a Texas lake. Texas has only one natural lake, Caddo, and that's half in Louisiana. Caddo Lake is exquisite in an exotic, moody, swamp-creature way. Every other lake in Texas is manmade, with varying degrees of aesthetic success. The tall cliffs and clear water of Possum Kingdom are inviting, but Joe Pool Lake in Dallas is a big puddle on the prairie. And I've never gotten used to the drowned trees that poke from Texas lakes, as if they never went down for the third time. These trees apparently provide places for bass to hang out and fishermen to find them, but they're dreary looking. There, I said it and I don't care who heard me.

Texas's rivers, on the other hand, are glorious. The old swimming holes about which old-timers wax nostalgic are crowded with cooler-packing crowds on weekends, but if you can sneak away on a weekday and rent a tube for a float down the Guadalupe, you will taste what Texas once was, what is still nearly within reach.

That Texas is worth seeing is nature's gift. That it offers much to keep tourists entertained is no happy accident. While some festivals have been around for decades, others, including the Fire Ant Festival, are recent inventions. In the 1980s the rallying cry for an economy that had just taken it in the knee-caps was "diversify" and diversify Texas did, with astonishing efficiency. The potential of tourism was identified, and as well as nurturing such established tourist destinations as Galveston Island and South Padre Island, the state saw to it that every little bend-in-the-road town pulled itself up by the bootstraps with bed and breakfasts, antique-and-teddy-bear shoppes, and festivals.

The East Texas town of Jefferson, thirty miles from the Louisiana border, is a particularly good example of how garden clubs and lemon-peach cinnamon French toast saved the state. Jefferson was a prosperous inland port in the nineteenth century, until the Corps of Engineers blew up a log jam on the Red River in 1873, diverting the river and ending Jefferson's port and glory days. The town spiraled into shabby gentility and out-right poverty. A century later, through the efforts of the Jesse Allen Wise Garden Club, the elaborate Victorian mansions built by shipping moguls became elaborate bed and breakfasts, and shops and restaurants returned prosperity to the town on the bayou.

Towns without lakes, rivers, Victorian mansions, or other obvious attributes rely on festivals celebrating whatever comes to mind: music, hummingbirds, black-eyed peas. Fall and spring weekends are fairs-and-festivals time, when city dwellers are advised to get out of town to check out some small-town action. At the Fire Ant Festival in Marshall, Texas, I ate alligator on a stick; shook hands with a toothy candidate for something or other; nearly bought a calico, cinnamon-scented stuffed bunny (before coming to my senses); and watched the parade, which included—as does every parade in Texas—Shriners in miniature cars. It was a typical Texas festival.

The German and Czech communities of Central Texas are big on celebrating wursts, polka, beer, and other old country imports with events like Wurstfest (Fredericksburg) and Westfest (West), and the Kolache Festival (Caldwell—a kolache is a pastry). The Hill Country town of Kerrville has one of the finest folk music festivals in the nation.

Juneteenth celebrations have sprung Texas borders and are spreading nationwide, though the event gives Yankee chicks pause. With all due respect, I am relieved that African-American Yankee chicks are as puzzled as I am over this celebration, which honors the day Texas slaves learned of their freedom—two years after the rest of the country. "That is the most bizarre holiday I've ever heard of in my life," says Melanie from Baltimore. "What is there to celebrate? It's not about celebrating 'cause you're free. It's really about celebrating because you're late." So, whatever, Texas blacks went ahead and made lemonade with what they were handed. It's a good party.

Much small-town tourist activity takes place in the squares surrounding Texas's magnificent courthouses. Texas has 254 counties and about 220 historic courthouses. These are elaborate, boastful buildings built in the flush of Victorian wealth with typical Texan braggadocio. The Texas Historic Courthouse Preservation Program (thanks, Dubya) provides millions of dollars in grants for courthouse preservation, and towns are going at it. You don't necessarily have to "set out" to see the courthouses—you stumble on them everywhere you go. Dallas has a chunky red stone Gothic affair; Marfa, deep in West Texas, is home to the imposing Presidio County courthouse; The Ellis County courthouse in Waxahachie is a stone Romanesque Revival structure built to last the next three millenniums. Old buildings surrounding the courthouse squares frequently are crammed with enough ye olde antique shops to kill a very happy Saturday afternoon (and a few husbands). Be warned, though, that some towns pretty much shut down on Sundays. In fact, "Blue Laws" prohibiting all sales on Sundays were repealed only in 1986.

The only downside of this successful transformation to a tourist economy is that in some ways, Texas has turned its very soul into a commodity. While Texans are rich again, Texas seems more self-conscious than it once was. With the influx of newcomers and tourists, Texas has become a show, a performance art version of Texas. The beer-swilling, butt-ugly sincerity of the old Texas honky-tonk scene ain't what it used to be. It was a Texas that made refined Yankees shudder, but I miss it, even though I share blame for its demise. That honky-tonk spirit has been diluted by the likes of me. "The whole jeans and boots and pickup truck thing in Texas.... I knew I could never be that but I admired it," says Holly from Oregon, wistfully. I want to be like that too, but the best I can do is wear the outfits and pretend. So you go to Gruene Hall, the oldest dance hall in the state, and there are me and Holly and Anne from Maryland with a bunch of her out-of-town Yankee friends, because this is one of the places she likes to bring visitors, and a bunch of German tourists in battered old cowboy hats they bought at a little West Texas shop that does a brisk business in battered old cowboy hats. We're all hooting like

Texans at the musicians on stage who are dressed in Western shirts and cowboy boots but are from Los Angeles. The whole scene is a reinterpretation of Texas honky-tonks. There are few real cowboys blowing off steam here. Just realtors in denim.

Is it all bad? At least we're keeping a version of the culture alive as everything around it changes, and it's always a helluvalot of fun to go out honky-tonkin'. I never learned how to drink beer until I puke, but I have learned how to go "WHOOOOOOOOO!" at the top of my lungs without embarrassment. The only thing I don't do, regretfully, is two-step. My husband and I have taken lessons, but we're too shy to get on the dance floor and practice, so we haven't mastered that smooth glide around the floor. Yankee chicks, if you've a mind, learn to dance. Then take yourself out to see some real Texas music. Hell, you can wear a cowboy hat if you want, nobody will care. Honky-tonks are often all-ages affairs, because grandma and grandpa still like to dance as much as the kids. It's amazing how the same dance steps look so different on everyone who does them, and how even the biggest-bellied cowboy-hatted old guys can dance like angels.

Or take a step back in the evolution of Texas honky-tonks and go to a Czech dance hall for a polka party. You haven't been to Texas until you've seen a full dance hall do the Chicken Dance. Even though you're there, it still has the taste of real Texas to it.

And with the explosion of tejano, homegrown Tex-Mex music, a whole new roots genre is opening up for exploration. Tejano music burst into the view of the nation with the 1995 murder in Corpus Christi of Selena. Marketers heard a giant KA-CHING in the outpouring of grief at the pop star's death, and tejano now has its own awards, charts, and videos, which I watch addictively even though I don't speak Spanish. (Most of them seem to be about a guy who really, really wants some sexy babe who spends a lot of time giving come-hither looks through cheesecloth.) Texas's Hispanic population has grown nearly 60 percent since 1990, and the Hispanic scene is on the cutting edge here.

Not long ago I went to a block party in my neighborhood. The event celebrated a neighborhood improvement project of the cobblestones-and-quaint-lamppost variety. The core crowd of about 150 people standing around with plastic cups of flat beer was 96 percent white, with a handful of "multicultural" movers and shakers tossed in. At the outskirts of the festivities, the Hispanic families that dominate the neighborhood stood by the police barriers and watched, uncertain whether they were welcome to join the party and whether they wanted to. When my husband and I got bored, we went for dinner at a nearby Mexican restaurant, and that's where we found the real party. The restaurant was jammed with everyone who wasn't at the street party—teenaged girls clutching teddy bears their dates bought from vendors who moved among tables; packs of young women getting chummily loopy together on margaritas; families from grandma to toddlers, who clutched balloon animals. A mariachi band big enough to circle a table of twelve strolled the cavernous rooms. Many of the musicians were young, dashing in black charro suits, and sang with strong, confident voices. I don't care what else was going on anywhere else in the city that night. People were having more fun here. This is what is happening in Texas today.

Hat Acts for Yankees

When German met Mexican met Irish met African-American on Texas soil, a rich musical slumgullion resulted. Music runs through the veins of Texans and is rich with ever-developing tradition, from cowboy yodels on the prairie to today's burgeoning tejano, which started to veer into American pop/ country in Spanish, but now is reaching back to lift up Mexican conjunto traditions. Now the accordion is cool in the U.S. for probably the first time ever.

Music was expression for immigrants dreaming of home and for otherwise taciturn cowboys lonely on the range. It was the lament of slaves, and the joy—long repressed, now bubbling forth again—of Mexicans at home. Music made Texas a less lonely place, and the music of Texas today is still where everyone comes together and has a party.

Traditionally, dance halls positioned themselves, like today's liquor stores, on wet/dry borders. This was where you went to have a drink and visit with your neighbors. Music was part of the experience, and it was a family affair. One old-timer told me about being tucked in under the table at a Central Texas dance hall to sleep while the adults drank and danced.

Willie Nelson, Blind Lemon Jefferson, Scott Joplin, Dale Evans, Lyle Lovett, George Strait, Buddy Holly, Janis Joplin, Steve Earle, Erykah Badu, Selena, Tex Ritter, Gene Autry, Earnest Tubb, Stevie Ray Vaughan, Tanya Tucker, Bob Wills are a stream-of-consciousness list of Texans who have risen to musical prominence. And songwriters have saluted Texas in dozens, maybe hundreds of songs: "Miles and Miles of Texas," "Across the Alley from the Alamo," "Deep in the Heart of Texas," "San Antonio Rose," "El Paso," "Does Fort Worth Ever Cross Your Mind," "Galveston," "Texas (When I Die)," "Luckenbach Texas," "Amarillo By Morning," "Dallas," "All My Ex's Live In Texas," "Abilene," "Big Balls in Cowtown." Texas even has a governmental department, the Texas Music Office, dedicated to spreading the word and bringing in the dollars of homegrown music.

Austin is home to "Austin City Limits," of course, and the South-by-Southwest conference, an annual music industry shmoozefest where the wannabes and hopefuls vie to be discovered and listen to panels of music pundits tell them how slim the chances are that they will be. (SXSW, like everything else in Austin, has grown, and old-timers complain about how pretentious it's gotten and how you can't get into clubs anymore to see any acts.) San Antonio is a mecca for tejano and home to the annual Tejano Music Awards.

Many Yankees have a negative knee-jerk reaction to country music, and that's a crying shame. The trouble is, the same forces that highjacked rock and turned it formulaic have gotten a stranglehold on country radio. But I have a hard time believing that even Yankees most hostile to country music would not be seduced into toe tapping if they heard country performed with all the sincerity that created it. Anyone who can remain unmoved by genuine Western Swing should perhaps enlist the help of a proctologist. If you hate country music, you've never heard it done right. Go hear good country music immediately. It's all around you.

This is just a minuscule selection of acts worth catching. They're all more true Texas than Nashville, so give them a try.

Asleep at the Wheel: Took over Western Swing where Bob Wills left off. Asleep at the Wheel is long-lived, beloved, and perpetually almost famous.

Dale Watson: Tattooed and truckin' honky-tonk hero.

Steve Earle: Though settled in Nashville, still Texas's answer to Bruce Springsteen.

Tish Hinojosa: Bordertown chanteuse who wraps a strong and lovely voice around songs in English and Spanish.

The Flatlanders: Band whose sole album is titled *More a Legend Than a Band* gets together from time to time when members Butch

Hancock, Jimmie Dale Gilmore, and Joe Ely feel like it. The sound is high-lonesome alt-country.

Jerry Jeff Walker: Guitar-based classic country rockin' that makes people holler.

Ray Wylie Hubbard: Country, folky, honky-tonky. Hoot 'n' holler.

Robert Earl Keen: Such a charming songwriter and storyteller, his large and loyal following forgives his less-than-stellar voice.

Brave Combo: OK, they're not cowboys, but they are polka, and that's true Texas, too. Where Brave Combo goes, parties break out.

Junior Brown: He makes other guitar players weep with envy.

Guy Clark: Now among the elder statesmen of the singer/songwriter/storyteller genre.

Ramon Ajala: Modern tejano pop idol.

> **Little Joe y Familia:** Old-school tejano.
> **Toni Price:** Yankee chick who moved to Austin via Nashville. Bluesy, blue-grassy, jazzy, and has Keith Richards' name tattooed on her arm. ♦

Much of historic Texana has been watered down into bandana print-trimmed bluebonnet paintings, but the good news is, you can still be appalled and astounded now and then if you like. Newspapers break out in Yankee v. Texan hostilities annually over the Sweetwater Rattlesnake Roundup, a grisly tradition since 1958. Holly went to the Roundup many years ago, and it remains an important moment in her Texification. Although she's lived in Texas twenty years now, she still sees this event from across a divide.

Basically, she explains, they get a bunch of rattlesnakes and throw them by the garbage canful into a big pit. Then the Rattlesnake Roundup Queen gets in the pit and walks among the snakes while they strike at her boot-protected ankles. "Then they skinned the rattlesnakes right there and hung up these giant skins. The skins continued to move for a while." Holly shuddered. This small-town festival remains stubbornly unfriendly to the casual tourist and a bone of contention between Texans and outsiders.

"Where you from, Steve?" wrote a Texan, in response to a letter in the newspaper calling the festival barbaric. "Have you not been here long enough to learn we poor ignorant Texans couldn't understand your upscale New York thinking? ... The local economy is supplemented by tourism ... Let nature take its course!" Texans consider themselves a force of nature. If you've ever debated their ways with them, you might agree.

The State Fair of Texas also wears traces of the past, but in a more gentle fashion. I have attended every fair since moving to Texas. Tom and I call the fair "butts and guts" because of the high concentration of proud beer guts and bodacious Texas chick butts crammed into painted-on Rocky Mountain jeans, the brand preferred by genuine Texas kicker chicks. Visit the animal barns, where proud 4-H-ers, all freckles and Adam's apples, tend their livestock lovingly, hoping for blue ribbons. (Then they say good-bye as prize-winning beef is auctioned off for slaughter, a staple among news tearjerker stories around fair time.)

The most committed fairgoers are in it for the food, which is deliciously greasy and unhealthy. My friend John, a nearly lifelong Dallas boy until he finally realized his dream and moved to Austin after retiring, insists on going to the fair each year on opening day because that's when the grease is fresh and his corny dog has not been fried in the grease of a thousand others. Houston's Livestock Show and Rodeo and Fort Worth's Southwestern Exposition Livestock Show and Rodeo offer the same sort of down-home entertainment and good bad food. (Rodeos, by the way are fun to a point. They are entertaining cultural excursions into the land of cowboy hats, and events like barrel racing can be exciting to watch. But rodeos also have a high pain quotient. Try a rodeo once. You'll be glad you saw it; you may or may not ever want to see another.)

Keep in mind that wherever you live in Texas, Texas is more than that. I'm a little shocked by the number of Yankee chicks who always head straight for the airport when they have some time off, and I urge them to spend some time exploring Texas instead. "It *is* like a whole other country," says Ellen from New York, which is what the tourist board tells us. In a way, it's true. Check it out.

Blame John Wayne: The Alamo

Ellen and her daughter were less than reverent when visiting the Alamo. They even giggled a little. "One of the docents overheard us and told us that we were on sacred ground and if we weren't appropriately respectful, we would have to leave," she says.

Yankee chicks don't "get" the Alamo.

"I didn't know until I read Texas history that John Wayne and the rest of them lost," says Melanie from Maryland.

Here is the Cliff's Notes on the Alamo: Texas was fighting for independence from Mexico. James Bowie, Davy Crockett (played by John Wayne in the movie), and a small militia of about 184 people defended the Alamo from a Mexican army of thousands under the command of General Antonio López de Santa Anna. All the Texians (pre-statehood Texans) except a few women and children died, but the thirteen-day battle gave Sam Houston, military commander of the Republic of Texas, time to prepare for the Battle of San Jacinto, where soldiers hollered "Remember the Alamo!" (and "Remember Goliad," but that's another story) as they charged. The Battle of San Jacinto turned the tide of the fight for independence, and Texans have been feverishly remembering the Alamo ever since.

Note that the men who died at the Alamo were not actually Texans. Davy Crockett and his militia were from Tennessee but came down to support the battle of independence from Mexico. In the John Wayne movie, Wayne, as Davy Crockett, tried to explain why.

"I like the sound of the word," he says. "It means people can live free, talk free, go or come, buy or sell, be drunk or sober, however they choose. Some words give you a feeling. 'Republic' is one of those words that makes me feel tight in the throat."

Wayne/Crockett continues in this vein, and by the time he gets to the day his "first baby shaves" and "makes his first sound like a man," he's lost me entirely. Perhaps Texans know what he's talking about. I haven't a clue.

I usually keep my opinion of the Alamo to myself because nothing I say goes over well among Texans. For example, I'm not sure I think it was so smart for those soldiers to stand firm in the face of certain death. Even more heinous, it's hard to shake the question about whether the sacred cause these soldiers fought for was the right to take what wasn't theirs. That statement is pure sacrilege in Texas and a clear sign of how little I know and understand of Texas history. But in order to fully appreciate the heroism and sacrifice of the Alamo story, you have to swallow any reservations you might have about the concept of Manifest Destiny, and remember that the egotism and unsavory dealings of Mexican president Santa Anna were part of the problem for Texians and some Mexicans as well. And this all happened before

we had the United Nations, and the whole world at
this time was running around claiming bits of turf for
themselves. The Battle of the Alamo was about the
courage to stand until the end for what you believe in
against all odds. That's what gets Texans misty-eyed.

Then, of course, there's the John Wayne factor.

I was blubbering by the end of the movie, *The
Alamo*. Who could steel her heart against the last
scenes, with that motley militia raising its rifles with
more bravado than brains against a wall of Santa
Anna's troops approaching, uniforms sparkling,
bugles bugling, cannons booming? It's exceptional
Western kitsch and deserves a great deal of credit for
establishing the story of the Alamo in the national
consciousness. "It's bad history...maybe bad
cinema, but I love the story of heroism and sacrifice it
tells," said one Alamo historian in *The Dallas Morning
News*. Wiping away tears, I can only agree, like
millions of other people.

Equally responsible for keeping the misty myths in
the minds of Texas is the Daughters of the Republic of
Texas, who have been officially responsible for
prompting our memories of the Alamo since 1861.
"People worldwide continue to remember the Alamo
as a heroic struggle against overwhelming odds—a
place where men made the ultimate sacrifice for
freedom. For this reason the Alamo remains
hallowed ground and the Shrine of Texas Liberty,"
DRT literature intones.

With John Wayne and the DRT standing guard,
the myth of the Alamo has held strong for decades,
but in recent years it has come under siege by

historians challenging the sentimental details—and a few larger points—of the story, such as exactly what inspired the militia to fight. Some say it was because Texas would join the Union as a slave state, tipping the balance of the Union. Some say it was because Santa Anna tried to stem the flow of Anglo immigration to the region, which adds an ironic twist. Many of the heart-stirring tales that have woven themselves around the siege of the Alamo are also under fire. We know Travis probably didn't draw a line in the sand with his sword as the Mexican army approached, over which he invited all who would stay and fight to step. We know James Bowie did not die in a fall from a platform while he was positioning a cannon; he got a bullet through the brain while he lay in bed, where he was confined with tuberculosis. And perhaps most shocking, a diary reportedly belonging to one of Santa Anna's soldiers claims that Davy Crockett did not die in battle but was taken captive and executed. True believers pish-posh the notion, and some archivists and historians are appalled and debate the diary's authenticity, but they have yet been able to debunk or to verify it.

The *San Antonio Express-News* tried to soothe readers who were depressed by this diary's claim in an unsigned editorial "More important for those who cherish the heroic memory of Crockett, de la Peña never says that Crockett surrendered," the editorial says comfortingly. "According to his account, Crockett died an even more brutal death than had been thought. He was tortured and hacked with swords and bayonets. Where and how Crockett drew his last breath does not diminish his legend or his honor." In other words, as long as Crockett died miserably and in pain, he retains hero stature. (See "The Lord is My Quarterback, I Shall Not Fumble: Football" page 89.)

Like the story of Christopher Columbus, the legend of the Alamo is taking a beating. But I think the Alamo will emerge triumphant after the dust settles. The men of the Alamo stood behind their beliefs to the very end, and you have to admire that. The truth may not be exactly as John Wayne told it, but it's a ripping yarn anyway. ✦

Chapter Six

Workin' Hard or Hardly Workin'?

"When I first arrived from New York City, I told people I felt like I'd retired."

—Dana, New York, six years in Texas

S ay *la dolce vita* with a twang, and that's the
Texas life.

I decided to move to Texas after visiting friends in Fort
Worth several times over a period of years. What I best recall
about those visits is sitting under a big tree on their deck, a cold
drink in hand, jawing from early afternoon until it was time to
throw a hunk of flesh on the grill for dinner. That was enough to
make me sublet my New York flat, pack a VW Rabbit full of crap
I couldn't live without, and drive southwest. Now I have my
own Texas tree, and as my husband and I frequently sigh to
each other as we lounge beneath it, "Dis is da life!"

Yankee chicks capable of slowing down love the pace and
style of Texas. "I've been out of New York long enough that I'm
not so uptight and closed-minded about some of the differences
down here," says Karen. "It's laid back and relaxed. People
move in slow motion."

Except on the highways, Texans are in no all-fired hurry.
Nobody ever feels compelled to get anything done in a "New
York minute," as it's known down here. They know the value of
a brisket smoked for hours until it's rich as chocolate; of a summer day squandered bobbing down a chilly river on an inner
tube; of a long buildup full of leisurely digressions in a story; of
an afternoon in the dim and soothing cool of a San Antonio
hole-in-the-wall where you order your beers in Spanish.
(Happy hour is not a Texas phenomenon, but I contend that
happy hour in Texas is happier. There's a chemical reaction
between heat, cold beverage, and late afternoon sunshine that
makes me very, very happy.)

Life is slower and getting things done is easy. "It's easy to get around. It's easy to park. You can find a place to buy what you need. You can find what you want," says Cerie from L.A. And you can get there in the privacy of your own car. "I haven't taken a bus since I moved to Dallas because I don't have to," says Melanie from Baltimore with a guilty giggle.

One of the first things I noticed when I moved down is that even in the big cities, you could go to a restaurant and your chair didn't touch anyone else's. These days I get the heebie-jeebies after a week in New York because I'm no longer accustomed to being in such close proximity with so many bodies. A memory I dwell on when homesick for the Old Country: Being crammed into an overheated city bus, wrapped in winter woolies, clutching a strap, bodies pressed against me, the hot breath of a stranger on my neck, while the bus lurches and groans through evening rush hour. Makes me queasy to think of it.

Here, you have space. Lots of space, both public and private. Although my financial situation is no better than the rest of my family, I am the first to own my own home. What is not possible in New York, L.A., or Chicago is possible in Texas cities, and what is not possible in Texas cities is possible in the 'burbs and small towns.

And if you can get a lot of house for the buck, you can get even more house for more bucks. Texas is full of people's ideas of dream houses. Rambling homes of Austin stone, pseudo-Tudors in tony gated communities, McMansions jammed onto ever-shrinking lots so that Texans can live comfortably with everything they want. Texans don't scrimp on themselves.

Some Famous People Born in Texas

Alvin Ailey, modern dancer, Rogers
Mary Kay Ash, pink-hued cosmetics mogul, Hot Wells
Clyde Barrow, infamous gangster, Telico
Carol Burnett, beloved comedienne, San Antonio
Cyd Charisse, leggy dancer, Amarillo
Joan Crawford, scary movie star, San Antonio
Farrah Fawcett, blonde sex goddess, Corpus Christi
Larry Hagman, actor who personified Dallas, Fort Worth
Don Henley, Eagle, Dallas
Ima Hogg, philanthropist at whose name you dare not
    giggle, Mineola
Buddy Holly, bespectacled country pop icon, Lubbock
Howard Hughes, peculiar millionaire, Houston
Lyndon Baines Johnson, colorful U.S. president,
    Stonewall
Janis Joplin, 1960s pop icon, Port Arthur
Scott Joplin, ragtime genius, Linden
Mary Martin, Peter Pan impersonator, Weatherford
Don Meredith, football player and discusser, Mt. Vernon
Ann Miller, toothy dancer, Houston
Willie Nelson, grizzled country singer, Abbott
Roy Orbison, crooner in dark glasses, Wink
Bonnie Parker, gangster moll, Rowena
H. Ross Perot, U.S. presidential wannabe, Texarkana
Katherine Anne Porter, short story genius, Indian Creek
Dan Rather, talking head, Wharton

Robert Rauschenberg, pop artist, Port Arthur
Gene Roddenberry, Trekkie hero, El Paso
Nolan Ryan, baseball icon, Refugio
Ann Sheridan, glamorous movie star, Denton
Willie Shoemaker, small man who rode fast horses, Fabens
Sissy Spacek, otherworldy movie star, Quitman
George Strait, cowboy crooner, Pearsall
Tommy Tune, lanky dancer, Wichita Falls
Bob Wills, Western Swing inventor, Kosse
Babe Didrikson Zaharias, athlete extraordinaire, Port Arthur
ZZ Top musicians Frank Beard, Billy Gibbons, and Dusty Hill, excessively bearded rock stars, Houston, Dallas, Waxahachie

Born elsewhere but got here as fast as they could then left

Walter Cronkite, Most Trusted Man in America, Houston
Donald Bartheleme, postmodern novelist, Houston
Jayne Mansfield, bosomy movie goddess, Dallas

Born elsewhere but got here as fast as they could and stayed

Donald Judd, minimalist artist, Marfa
Robert James Waller, tearjerker writer, Alpine
Sandra Bullock, America's Sweetheart, Austin ✦

"My bathroom is bigger than my first apartment," says Mary. "In Manhattan, it would probably rent for $2,000 a month. It's a modest example of what I call the 'Texas Grooming Shrine.' Some of them are so opulent and gilded, you feel you need to genuflect when you enter. Mine's not fancy but it's big."

"I've been surprised by how many Texans I've met who seem vaguely independently wealthy," says Jennifer, who lived in several states before settling in Texas nine years ago. "People have horses, land, ranches! And some of them tend to follow their dreams without a steady job while owning houses that it takes my family two incomes to afford."

Beth from Indiana says, "We still have the sofa my husband remembers abusing when he was growing up." When Beth buys a new sofa, she will be a step closer to being Texan. Why scrimp on yourself? is the Texas credo. Enjoy! While Texans may be conservative politically overall, fiscally they believe in making money and spending money.

The entrepreneurial code of Texas says it's better to try and fail than never to have tried at all. "This is still the land where everything is assumed to be possible," Molly Ivins wrote, even after the oil bust. Texas is friendly to business (a mixed blessing), and entrepreneurs with ideas thrive here. "The attitude is, 'Hey, I got rich and you can too! There's enough for everyone!'" says Mary. If you try and fail, you pick yourself up and start over again. Texas is proud of its high-dollar success stories, like Tomima Edmark, who created a hair gizmo called the Topsy Tail that made her millions; Ross Perot, who started EDS on a $1,000 loan from his wife; and Mary Kay Ash, who leveraged cosmetics, personality, and a pink Cadillac into a sales force of more than 750,000. (See "I Am Woman Hear Me Jangle," page 163.)

And while we don't have the Met or Carnegie Hall or the Chicago Art Institute, perhaps because choice is more limited, I have found myself doing things I might never have done in New York. I might never have gotten around to seeing the late raconteur Quentin Crisp, but he was in town, I wanted an evening's entertainment, tickets were affordable, and I had a great time. And I probably wouldn't have suffered the effort to see Madonna's Like A Virgin tour at Madison Square Garden, but going to Reunion Arena was easy and it was back when I could afford Madonna tickets. I saw Garth Brooks, before he was all that he is, in an old honky-tonk in Lancaster; and Bill Monroe on a bill with the Dixie Chicks before they became all that they are. I most assuredly would not have seen country legend George Jones three times had I stayed in New York, but I'm proud that I have. (The evil twin of all this is that I probably would never have gone to see Debbie Reynolds in *The Unsinkable Molly Brown*, in New York, but I was in Dallas, somebody offered me tickets, so I went. It was a long evening.)

Here, you also have the leisure and opportunity to create the life you want for yourself. With less external stimuli clamoring for your attention, you must find your own entertainment. The do-it-yourself culture can be broadening. Linda, from Ohio via Detroit, finds that in Dallas she's inspired to participate in arts she'd only watched before. "In other places those things are there for me—the music, the arts. I could go see them and be around them. I didn't have to be as motivated to do them myself. Here, I realized, I'm gonna have to do it myself. I'm studying African drama, playing African drum, gotten hands-on involved instead of just going and listening."

Artists start galleries and museums (in Dallas, the McKinney Avenue Contemporary, known as the MAC, was started by a group of local artists disgruntled by the conservative bent of the Dallas Museum of Art; in Houston, the Orange Show Foundation, which supports the arts of everyday people, grew from the Orange Show Monument, built by postal worker Jeff McKissack, who had an idea, although nobody is quite sure what that was); musicians build studios in their garages and record albums; business people start businesses then sell them and start another; pastors establish churches in shopping centers and build a congregation, which then builds a church building of its own. If you can dream it, you can do it, and nobody here is ever accused of dreaming too big. Nothing is too big for Texas.

It's funny, then, that along with this entrepreneurial verve, Texas business also moves at a leisurely pace that makes fast-moving Yankees twitch.

"When I was in D.C., and in college, I was kind of middle of the road," says Anne. "I wasn't one of those obsessively obsequious people whose whole goal was to get ahead in life. I wanted to enjoy myself. Now I come down here, suddenly I'm considered aggressive. I don't think they know what to do with me sometimes."

"I think because the cost of living is so low in Texas, people are not very motivated to work hard," says Maria, who has trouble keeping her sushi restaurant staffed. "In Seattle it's probably going to take an income and a half to make it, so people work very hard. People are always on the move, and they don't really complain about putting in an extra hour here and there. Here, I find if they can make ends meet and have a little bit left over, they're happy. If I ask an employee to cover another shift because someone called in sick, chances are they're going to say no. Once you set their shifts, it's very difficult to ask them to change. At first I thought that was kind of strange, then I got used to it. They have a relaxed attitude, like, 'even if I don't work for two or three days I can get by, so maybe I should go fishing today.'"

And because many families apparently can afford to get by on one salary, many do. "I'm surprised here in Austin how many women don't work," says Holly. "I never really considered that. It's just so much a part of my fabric."

"Since there's no pressure socially to work, I don't," says Mary. "But I went to a spa with a bunch of friends from the East Coast and I felt like such a slacker. Up there, there's more pressure to work. You feel more out of it if you don't have a career."

Here—for women especially—careers are take it or leave it, and those who choose to leave it live stigma-free lives of different endeavors: raising children, volunteering, taking care of busy spouses. One friend of mine spent the first twenty-three years of her working life at the newspaper, scrambling to get the big bylines, the front page stories that spell status in the news business, the scoops, the stories behind the stories. But when in her mid-forties she became exhausted and disillusioned, and with a nice nest egg tucked away, she quit her job to rethink her life. After more than a year, she's still thinking. At the moment, the best thing she can think of doing is nothing much. "I'm a housewife," she says blissfully. "I cook, I clean. I love it."

This life is not about laziness, but priorities. Texas priorities lean towards time with the family, Friday night football and Sunday morning church, cold beer on a hot day and hot chili on a cold night. It's all simple stuff but can be awfully satisfying if you give it a chance.

My New York friends, living tantalizingly close to other people's fame, all have visions of bantering with Letterman dancing in their heads. (And yes, I confess to imagining my moments in the spotlight myself. Old habits die hard.) Texans who nurture those kinds of dreams tend to move to the coasts. Generally, Texans living outside the feverish quest for fame are likely to work only as hard as is required to live the good life as they see it. For some, that's a matter of earning just enough money to get by. For others, it requires enough income to buy and maintain a house big enough for the Von Trapp family and the Brady Bunch combined, a swimming pool, a boat, and two SUVs. Either way, jobs are more means to the end than the end itself. Here, if you have a career, that's great. Go forth and make a mess o' money and spend it on luxury as you see it. If you don't burn with ambition, no big deal. Have another glass of iced tea and relax. That's *la dolce vita,* y'all.

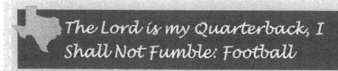

The Lord is my Quarterback, I Shall Not Fumble: Football

Football is Texas's third religion, after Southern Baptist and Catholic. After the prayer, the morality play begins. Players fight through adversity until they cross a line into success. Football victories are not ambiguous. They are definitive. Might makes right. Nice guys finish last.

Football is so deeply ingrained in Texas, teasing out the reasons is difficult. The explanations go 'round and 'round and 'round. Why is football religion? Because Texans worship football. Why do Texans worship football? Because football is a religion. Football madness starts with high school football and continues through the pros, astonishing and baffling Yankee chicks.

"I have always been a football fan," says Judy from Pennsylvania. "But I don't remember any high school stadiums at home with Astroturf, elaborate concessions, and sold-out season tickets. Parents talk about showing up at 5 a.m. on ticket day and still not getting tickets. The stands are filled with adults who no longer have school-aged children. At Highland Park High School, 50-yard-line seats are reserved for adult season ticket holders, and the student section is down on the 10-yard line. When I went to high school, the students got the 50-yard-line seats."

One way to appreciate what football means to Texans is to drive out to Oil Spill, West Texas, get out of your car, look around, and try to figure out what you would do there every Friday night for the rest of your life. "I have to have something to look forward to, or life is just blah..." says one man in H.G. Bissinger's Yankee's-eye view of Texas high school football, *Friday Night Lights*. "...football helps you survive all this sand, the wind, the heat. I wouldn't live any other place."

High school football unites the people within towns and—in the way of rivalries—people in scattered towns. It is a web across Texas, connecting people of the huge state. Everyone turns up for Friday night football: kids and parents and grandparents, alumni and football scouts. The Permian Panthers, the team profiled in *Friday Night Lights*, attract upwards of 10,000 people to its games. Little towns on the prairies have plenty of room for high school football stadiums and build big fancy ones. High school pep rallies are high-decibel frenzies, with coaches hollering about butt-kicking into the megaphone, cheerleaders flipping hair and bodies, and everyone singing along to the team fight song.

My husband, who played football as a youngster in Kewanee, Illinois, was aghast when he moved to Texas at fifteen and attended his first Texas pep rally—so unlike the diffident affairs back in Illinois— and saw his new school's behemoth team. "It's like they're breeding football players here," he says. Chicago, where Tom's roots lie, is a football town but it's also a basketball and baseball town, like many northern cities. For a long time Texas was essentially a one-game state and even now, while basketball, baseball, and hockey are gaining ground, football remains The Sport. The others are also-rans.

Texans are rabidly loyal to their high school and college teams, although they are tough to please and outspoken. Even high school players are subjected to harsh scrutiny, but they take it because they also get the glory—the prettiest girls (see "Every Woman's Dream, Every Man's Fantasy: Cheerleaders," page 157), the cheers of thousands, lovingly painted paper banners to break through when they run on to the field. College scouts from all over the country come to Texas to recruit, and the adulation follows the youths into college—although high school stars who choose out-of-state colleges are not looked on kindly.

I know one guy in his sixties who goes to every single game the University of Texas Longhorns play even though he never even attended the school. That kind of commitment to the UT team is known as "bleeding orange." At UT's biggest rival, Texas A&M, the 12th Man tradition has fans stand through the entire game—ostensibly to rush onto the field should the team need them. And one Dallas woman had to plan her wedding around the Texas-OU game. "According to my beloved fiancé, this game is, and always will be, one of the most important days of his life!" she says. (Texas-OU is UT v. University of Oklahoma. The game is played in Dallas, which is halfway between the two schools, and surrounded by an infamously beer-soaked party.)

Football lets men prove their manliness, which seems to require pain and danger in the Texas tradition. In *Urban Cowboy*, nothing made Debra Winger look hornier than watching John Travolta do things that hurt, like ride the mechanical bull or get punched. Pain is manly and football requires pain. The first five minutes of *North Dallas Forty*, based on author Peter Gent's life as a Dallas Cowboy, when Nick Nolte puts his aging, aching body slowly into motion while recalling the hits of the previous day's game, is excruciating to watch. Maternal instinct kicked into high in women all over Texas when poor Troy Aikman started looking increasingly addled after his tenth concussion. We were all relieved when he retired.

"Football *hurts*," says a native-Texas friend who still rankles over the censure suffered when he finally admitted to himself he hated playing high school football and quit the team. "But you're looked down on if you don't play, and you don't even hope to date the best girls."

Texans who don't worship at the shrine of the pigskin sometimes have a violent contrary reaction. One of the godfathers of Texas letters, J. Frank Dobie, wondered, "Who believes that God cares whether one bunch of young apes or another one has the most success with an inflated pig bladder." And the most odious character in McMurtry's *The Last Picture Show* is the sadistic Coach Popper.

But these are counter-culture views. More common is the puzzlement of legendary high school coach Gordon Wood who couldn't imagine why any young man wouldn't want to hurl himself around on Astroturf. "I see some big ol' boy walking down the hall and I have to ask myself why he's not doing anything but attending class and hanging around in the JRB Food Store parking lot in the afternoon while some 140-pounder is out there with us, sweating and hurting," Wood said in Carlton Stowers' collection of articles, *Friday Night Heroes.*

The Yankee chick immediately knows the answer to this question: Because the big ol' boy apparently is not as dumb as he looks. But don't bother saying that aloud. A reader from Teaneck, N.J., responded to this Stowers article by suggesting that "subjecting seventeen-year-old boys to such pressures (not to mention some writer having gall enough to glamorize it!) deserved [a] rank right up there with Original Sin...!" Stowers reports, with an implied folksy chuckle. Texas boys throw themselves onto the football field because they are well rewarded. Football dreams dance in their heads—dreams of money, glory, state championships, Super Bowl rings, and parties like in *North Dallas Forty*, where beautiful cheerleaders grow up into luscious women eager to make a "quarterback sandwich" with Mac Davis. Football is a religion in Texas because Texans love everything about it, from the tailgate party to the post game show.

I tried to fit in by mustering up an interest in football but was unsuccessful. I suffer from a strange phenomenon when I sit in front of a football game. My eyes might be pointed at the television screen but I see nothing. My football zone is the twilight zone. And no matter how many times people have tried to explain "first downs" to me, I still don't get it. My husband won't even let anyone try anymore. "It's hopeless," he tells helpful friends. "Forget it."

But football season does have benefits for otherwise uninterested Yankee chicks. If your sig oth is a football fan, you're free on Sunday afternoons for the duration of the season. On Sunday afternoons, the roads are empty, parks are tranquil, stores and malls are full of happy football widows.

Or, since you can't hope to beat 'em, you can join 'em. Football is great casual entertaining, and I am happy to invite people over to watch whatever game they think is important at the moment (see "B.Y.O.M.," page 207). I buy chips and beer, cook up a pot of something good, and ignore the game entirely. There's a lot of down time in televised football that can be used for socializing. If you tape an NFL game and fast-forward through commercials, actual play time is something like 7½ minutes.

The Yankee chick football fan is advised to know and respect the rivalries. Don't sit in a crowd of Cowboys fans wearing a Redskins cap, or at a UT game wearing an A&M cap. Don't jeer UT in a crowd wearing the school's burnt orange. One native-Texan friend of mine, a pillar in the PTA and a UT fan, nearly came to blows with a University of Miami fan during a game. "She's the one who started bad-mouthing, so I told her that the Miami players were a bunch of dirty ball players," my friend explained. "She told me her husband said the UT players kept hitting their players out of bounds. I said at least I could watch the game without having to ask my husband what was going on.

"For the record, I am not normally belligerent, but it was cold, there was no hot water for coffee, I paid $175 for the tickets, we were getting our butts whipped, AND she had a stupid little hurricane painted on her cheek."

You've been warned. I'm not sure even a tough New York City chick could whup a Texas chick all hopped up on football.

Chapter Seven

Fixin' to Stop Making Sense

"I don't say 'fixin' to.' Shoot me in the head before I say that."

—Pat, Massachusetts, and
Beth, Indiana, both seven years in Texas

*T*he other day in the car, I turned to Tom and said, "Look at that big ol' new development back there."

Say what?

I've reached a point of no return. I'm talkin' Texan. Sometimes I sound ridiculous.

But Texas-talk is irresistible. When Ann Richards warned Walter Cronkite that she was going to "talk Texan" at the 1988 Democratic National Convention, she meant she'd be straying from the straight and narrow English language into a slipsy, slidey, colorful lexicon that never lets literal usage or grammatical purity get in the way of making a point. Ann Richards talked Texan on national TV and became America's sweetheart because talking Texan is fun.

And talking Texan is a creeping condition. It starts with y'all. According to my informal Yankee chick's research, "y'all" is the second-most adopted Texanism, after Tex-Mex, even though folks back home are horrified to hear it. The first time I let "y'all" slip in front of my mother, her hair stood on end. "Don't say that," she shuddered. "It sounds so ignorant."

"You guys" sounds better?

In no time at all, most Yankee chicks let "y'all" roll off their tongues like they were born in Lubbock. "I love saying y'all," Linda from Pennsylvania says, almost fervently. Y'all is easy, convenient, expedient. Be aware, however, that there are rules to it. "Yankees think they are being awfully cute when they tiptoe up to one lone southerner and say: 'How are youall today?'" Florence King wrote. "They can't get it through their heads that this word is *plural only*. The English language needs two forms of the second person, and southerners are the only

Americans who have both..." (There is little to explain the use of "all y'all" then, beyond an excess of generosity. Personally, I don't approve of that clearly ungrammatical usage.)

While the grammar is the same, note that King, who was born into an old Virginia family, uses the Southern "youall" as compared to a Texas "y'all," pronounced "yawl." Pronunciation does count. "I can't make myself say y'all because it sounds like you all and that is so *wrong*," says Laura. (Similarly, *The New Yorker* proved how clueless Yankees can be when an article described a man raised by Texans insisting his own children call him "sir" and their mother "madam." Oy. The proper Texas term is "ma'am" and the first time someone calls you that—and they will—is an unsettling rite of passage for women leaving youth for adulthood in Texas.)

The ultra-Texan "fixin' to" is used by most Yankee chicks only in implied ironic quotes. "I've heard a voice that sounds like mine say that about three times in the seven years I've lived in Texas, but I'm sure it's not me who's saying it," says Beth from Indiana. Only one Yankee chick I know embraces the phrase. "I love 'fixin' to,'" says Lisa from Indianapolis. "It's the ultimate in laid-back laziness. You don't actually have to do anything, you're just *fixin'* to."

A few other hardcore Texanisms slip out of Yankee mouths from time to time, but they don't all fit. "I told my husband I would try to use 'might could,' and I did try to say it a few times, but he said it really doesn't work on me," says Andrea from Oregon.

Otherwise, most Texanisms are fun and easy, and you're welcome to jump right in. Among my favorites is the use of "puny." If, for example, you were up too late and drank one-too-many margaritas on Saturday night, chances are good you would spend Sunday feeling puny. Puny is not exactly sick, it's just a kinda wan, a little off, slightly indisposed. Puny.

The expanded meaning of visiting is also fun. You can visit on the telephone or visit with someone about a particular issue as in, "I'd like to visit with you a minute about scheduling my vacation time this summer."

My friend Jenny (or maybe it's Ginny, I can't tell the two names apart in Texas) says her nephew is "tootie" when he's acting fussy. Love it, use it. Pam likes "right larripin'," which means terrific. Ginnie from Ohio was offended when a Texan looked at her firstborn and declared him "a mess" until she learned it was meant with affection.

Texas/Southern idioms are most fun of all. I like saying "rode hard and put up wet" when someone appears worn out. "Put up" itself is a new one for me—it means to put something away. I like "She's dumber than a box of rocks," "He don't have the sense God gave a goose," and "drunker than Cooter Brown" even though I don't know who Cooter Brown is nor does anyone else. I've also been known to tangle with "nervous as a long-tail cat in a room full of rocking chairs," though that one doesn't easily roll off the tongue of a fast-talking New Yorker. I'm sure I've said, "a room full of long-tail rocking chairs" on occasion.

Sometimes syntax takes a twist. When I first moved down, I was confused by Texans' tendency to use "I tell you what" at the end of sentences instead of the beginning, so that they had in fact already told me "what" by the time they got around to telling me they were going to tell me "what." They would say "I tell you what" and I would be poised for more, but nothing was forthcoming. It's a Texas thing, I got used to it.

You understand, of course, that none of these conversational flourishes are fully acceptable in a Yankee accent. Sometimes I can actually feel my tongue exercising new muscles as—seemingly with a mind of its own—my New York honk evolves into Texas twang.

I dropped *pee*-can in favor of pa-*kahn* almost immediately. It sounds prettier and besides, Texans grow the nuts, they should decide how the name is pronounced. "*Ah*-ringe" is now "ahrnj." "*HAR*-ibble" is now "*whore*-ibble." Among the more shocking developments, the moment when I most feel like I'm morphing into Bubba: "doesn't" has slouched into "dudn'," "isn't" has become "idn'," and "then" seems to have picked up an extra syllable to become "they-an."

Extra syllables are a big player in talking Texan. Texans can stretch one common monosyllabic rant into five syllables. "*Sssshhhheeeeeiiiiiiiiit.*" "They make it about ten syllables," says Anne. "In New York, the word is quick and to the point. Texans turn it into an entire social commentary. Molly Ivins is a master at the word."

(Molly Ivins, by the way, in a stint at *The New York Times* in the 1970s, was discouraged from talking Texan in her writing. Copy editors actually changed "beer gut" to "protuberant abdomen" in one case, in a breathtaking display of leaden-handed editing.)

I've also stumbled upon pronunciation differences so subtle I can't always figure them out even after they are explained: Jenny/Ginnie, pen/pin. Who can tell the difference? One Texan friend laughs and laughs at his own imitation of me saying the name "Karen." I don't mind, but I have no clue what he's laughing about. To my ears, his imitation sounds nothing like me. "*KHA*-ren," he says, "*Haw, haw, haw. KHA*-ren."

Texans do talk funny, but it's crucial to remember *That's just the way they talk.* Don't kid yourself that everyone with a "Hee-Haw" accent is a yokel. The accent-as-reflection-of-worldliness is a notion contradicted by the people you will meet who sound like they never left the farm but who actually have traveled the world, have Ph.D.s, have work hanging in museums, or are president of the United States. It's hard to believe at first, but it's true. You'll get over it.

Texans also have a different conversational style. Yankee-style conversation is often layered, with one person's contribution overlapping the final words of the previous comment. "My family all talks at once," says Andrea from Oregon, who married a Texan. "But with my husband's family, the room is quiet and there are pauses after you speak. I hate how often I interrupt people. I'm trying to change that."

I, too, frequently backpedal off the tails of Texans' sentences. While a Yankee would keep talking right through my interruption, Texans politely stop talking and show me the courtesy I've neglected to show them. (Probably cutting me slack because I'm a Yankee and don't know better.) It's embarrassing, so I apologize and urge them to continue.

Though I must admit that a room full of people all honking opinions at once with flailing hands is one of the things I miss about Yankeeland. I suppose the Texas version of conversational style is storytelling, at which Texans excel and pride themselves. You see it done by all the most beloved Texas singer-songwriters. Guy Clark, Robert Earl Keane, the late Townes Van Zandt all owe their popularity to their ability to spin a yarn. I am a fan of many of these guys but confess never having slowed my internal clock enough to appreciate the master storyteller's long slow ramble. I'm not a good enough listener. I want to honk and flail. Maybe if I stay here another twenty years.

Another thing I miss is casual cussing, a few well-placed expletives to make my points more colorful. "It's just Yankee shtick," says Cerie from L.A.

I do let some juicy words slip sometimes, but in twenty years here, I've cleaned up my act considerably. On one visit to New York, I waited for a light behind a couple of well-groomed young professional women, whose conversation was peppered with the word "motherf***." This shocked me, and I was simultaneously shocked because I was shocked. "Motherf***" is a riper word than even I tangle with, but such loose profanity would have been easier to ignore had I never moved to Texas. My southern friend Christine, in a New York restaurant with her husband, noticed him looking uneasy. When she asked if he was OK, he said, "I'm not used to hearing f*** yelled all around me while I eat." On a recent trip to New York I was perversely tempted by a widely-sold souvenir T-shirt printed with the obnoxious yet liberating slogan: "F*** You You F***ing F***."

Casual obscenity, except for an occasional well-placed *ssshhheeeiiiiiiiiit*, just doesn't happen here and it doesn't go over. Pat once pulled a visiting Yankee colleague aside to advise him that in meetings, "You can't say 'f*** this' and 'f*** that.'" Barbara from Oregon actually had an employee take her aside and scold her. "Some of us are offended," the person said.

While all Yankees don't swear, of course, there is a contingent of us who can get blue. When Pat and I first met in Texas and realized we shared that bond, we relaxed into language that would make a gangsta rapper blush. It just felt good to let it rip a moment.

Texans like their language peppery, while at the same time maintaining a southern delicacy. Even when discussing Texans' attitudes towards things scatological in *In a Narrow Grave,* McMurtry refers to kids having their faces pushed into a "commode bowl." To my ears, a plain ol' toilet bowl sounds more disgusting and in a case like that, why be delicate? I've never been at ease with "commode," which sounds Victorian, although nowadays when I have to "go," I ask for the "rest room" or the "ladies' room." My Yankee-style "bathroom" now sounds inelegant to me, even crass.

So, you take some, you leave some. Talking Texan is one of the state's joys. You can't resist it if you stay here long enough. It creeps into your mouth and hijacks your tongue. Before you know it, you're saying "li'l ol' this" and "big ol' that." But be warned: It's a slippery slope. The other day, in front of a whole group of people, I opened my mouth and out came, "Blabbity blabbity, blabbity blabbity blab, *aiii tell yeeew whuuuuuut.*" I am too far gone to save now.

The White Socks: Bubbas and Good Ol' Boys

Texas is full of guys in white socks who have to decide whether to wear their pants over their beer guts or under. Some of these guys are Bubbas, some are Good Ol' Boys. While this is not an official distinction, it helps me differentiate between guys I like and guys I don't. Briefly, Bubba is the ignorant redneck that unenlightened Yankees think run the state. The Good Ol' Boy is a helpful, friendly, colorful character you want living next door to you.

Although Bubba doesn't have the clout he once did in Texas, he's hanging in there and you'll run into him from time to time. One of my favorite Bubba sightings was on the letters page of *The Dallas Morning News* when, in response to a Yankee's comment on something or other, Bubba griped about "overeducated Yankees" telling Texans what to do. That's pure Bubba, proud and obstinate about the Everyman nobility of ignorance. A couple of days later, a letter ran in response from a puzzled Yankee wondering what "overeducated" meant.

Bubba let out an indignant roar when the "no pass, no play" laws hit the books in 1984. The big beef was, of course, football. Book learning is fine but football is *football*. It's how Texas heroes are made. Nobody ever became famous in Texas by being an intellectual. McMurtry titled an essay on the region's literature "Southwestern Literature?"—with a question mark—and points out that the feeling that one ought to apologize for book learning was "a feeling one comes by naturally in the rural Southwest."

One legacy of this bit of Bubba-think is that it can be easy to sound like a smarty-pants down here. "I come down here and suddenly I'm using 'big words' I never thought were a big deal before," says Anne from Maryland. But as the state goes more high tech, the value of education is increasing in the eyes of Texas. Texas doesn't have much choice if it wants to continue the remarkable growth it's been seeing. But change is slow because Bubba is stubborn and would rather his high school build a new football stadium than a library.

Your personal encounters with Bubba will be contingent on the life you lead. Pam, who works at a university, says the only time she ever sees Bubba is in the letters page of the newspaper. Anne and Karen, reporters in San Antonio, both encounter Bubba in the course of their work. "Some of them can't do anything but flirt," says Anne. "I can't tell you how many old men come up to me and put their arm around me." I once had a woman, a Bubba-ette, plop down next to me at a Vietnamese-run nail salon and complain about how "these people" should learn to talk English if they're going to live in America. (I'm not sure what shocked me most—that she thought this way or that she considered it an acceptable sentiment to express to a stranger.) I was once startled by a dim-witted anti-Semitic remark from a Bubba teaching an ethics class at a small community college.

The legacy of Bubba is perhaps more troubling than the old goat himself. Bubba doesn't lynch anymore (the Jasper horror notwithstanding) but the bitter taste of that era remains. It's not long since one Texas town retired the sign that welcomed visitors to a town with "the blackest soil and the whitest people," and I still hear the "n" word more often than I care to.

Yankee chicks would be provincial to assume, however, that racial problems are greater here than back home. Of course, "back home" is enough different places that we cannot even treat Yankee chicks as a group in this context. Until I'd been to a McDonald's in Carrollton, Texas, I thought the company's TV commercials full of rosy, toothy, young blonde people in paper caps were pure fiction. But Laura and Melanie both moved to Dallas from Des Moines, Iowa, and are perfectly pleased with the city's diversity. "Des Moines was *really* white bread," says Laura.

And frankly, bigotry is a lot less jarring when the dialect is familiar. One problem with southern bigots is that they tap into one of Yankees' most deeply held bigotries: the southern redneck bigot. If you open a Yankee's mind-dictionary, the picture next to the word "bigot" would be of Bubba so Yankee chicks recoil at anyone resembling Bubba but perhaps are less fearful of more familiar characters who might be equally bigoted. Because of course you know Texas has not cornered the market on bigots. And you should know that the guy in that mind's-eye dictionary might not actually be Bubba. He might be a Good Ol' Boy.

Good Ol' Boys look like Bubba and sound like Bubba, but they are the kind of guys who, when they hear your gutter blew off in a storm, turn up with a ladder and tools and fix the thing without so much as a "you owe me." In *Urban Cowboy*, Bud's Uncle Bob was a Good Ol' Boy. He took Bud in, helped him find a job, taught him to ride the mechanical bull, and set him straight about the value of a good woman. Bud/John Travolta was a Bubba in most of the movie—popping Sissy one when she got out of hand, drinking too much, leering (if that's what you'd call that dopey look) at Jerry Hall and her sister while Sissy sat right beside him. But in the end, Bud takes his first steps towards Good Ol' Boyhood when he finally admits that he's stubborn and hotheaded but, "I love ya, Sissy." (My people would say that at that moment, he became a mensch.) On *King of the Hill*, the animated TV show based in a fictional Dallas 'burb, Hank Hill's daddy is Bubba. Hank Hill, however, is 100 percent Good Ol' Boy.

At the newspaper where I worked, the union shop where pages were assembled was a hotbed of Good Ol' Boys. I loved those guys. They teased me mercilessly about being a Yankee and pretended to complain every time I asked for help, but they always came through when I needed them, and they made me laugh with wisecracks muttered between goopy spits of tobacco juice into the cans they kept handy for that purpose.

Good Ol' Boys fix your car. They sell you your beer. They drag their riding mowers out to cut the lawn at your church. They help you figure out which one of about a gajillion bolts you need at the hardware store. Good Ol' Boys are a solid foundation of down-home good neighborliness in Texas.

The best and perhaps only way to tell if the guy with the beer gut and white socks is Bubba or a Good Ol' Boy is to get to know him. If he refers to any ethnic group by a slur, he's probably a Bubba. If he seems surprisingly gentle for a big guy dribbling a viscous brown liquid into a Dr Pepper can, he's a Good Ol' Boy.

The genuine Good Ol' Boy is a Texas treasure and long may he live. If you find yourself living next door to him, befriend him. Let him make fun of your Yankee ways, and let him teach you a thing or two about your garbage disposal, your transmission, your tomato plants. He loves to help little ladies like you.

Bubba, on the other hand, is probably following the cowboy and the wildcatter down the long, lonesome trail to Texas mythology. His power is waning. In Texas government, Bubba Bills, which *The Dallas Morning News* calls "plain laws for ordinary folk" and which usually "touch on the trademark elements: guns, alcohol, trucks, and livestock," are only colorful sidebars to politics these days. What the newspaper called "the ultimate Bubba bill—a state constitutional amendment to affirm the right of every Texan to hunt and fish"—didn't make it out of committee in 2001. Quintessential "anti-Bubba laws," as Ivins puts it, are seatbelt laws and the increasing stringency of open-container laws.

Bubba is less of a force than he once was. He's not running the state anymore, and while he can get on your last nerve with his ign'r'nt ways, I wouldn't spend much time worrying about him. Unless, of course, you're planning to run for sheriff of a small Texas town. ✤

Chapter Eight

Bless Your Heart, Aren't You Just the Most Precious Li'l Clod

"People were so nice when I moved down, I thought they all wanted tips."

—Mary, Ohio, twelve years in Texas

*T*exans' friendliness will charm you.

The natives' affability and good manners—among the traits that put the "south" in Southwest—grease the wheels of life here. Texans are right-out-there friendly, never shying away from neighborly chitchat. "Catch a person's eye, any person, any color, any age, any style—on the street, in an elevator, anywhere at all—and they nod, smile, and say 'Howareya,'" says Ginnie from Ohio. "I love that. A few weeks ago I was on my way to work one morning, late, feeling frazzled, and while I was stopped at a traffic light an old black man in a tattered straw hat and shabby denim overalls crossed the street in front of my car. 'Mornin,' he said with a big lovely smile, 'Gonna be a nice day.' 'Mornin',' I said back, 'I think you're right!' And I felt the delight of a real connection between two human beings who might as well have been from different planets."

Such promiscuous friendliness certainly is not the New York way. On my parents' first visit here, we spent an afternoon shopping neighborhood yard sales. As we browsed one place, I made small talk with the fellow killing an afternoon sitting in the driveway with his junk. My father was agog. "You were talking about the *weather*," he said. "You're a *Texan*."

On my first trip back after nine months in Texas, I stopped into a supermarket to pick up a few things. Already conditioned to Texas, I said "hi" to the cashier as I stepped up to the register. She looked at me as if I had belched.

And when they do speak, Yankees are far more likely to blast directly to the point than Texans. Once, as I waited in La Guardia Airport for a bus, I saw a cop approach a car stopped in a no-standing zone. What my Texas-trained ears were expecting to hear was, "Excuse me, but this is a bus stop. You can't stop here." What the cop bellowed was, "Get outta da bus stop." It was efficient, to the point, and effective. As a Yankee, I can appreciate that. But such efficiency is exactly the sort of behavior that makes Texans think us rude.

Texans say nothing without friendly digressions that can seem like meaningless, infuriating dalliances to Yankees. In *Southern Ladies and Gentlemen,* Florence King describes the trauma of a southern girl discussing an apartment rental with the landlord. "...my throat ached with unshed tears," she wrote. "He was not at all interested in standing around talking about this and that; he was not at all interested in my name; and worst of all, he did not ask me where I was from...he actually told me what the rent was before the first hour was up."

To Yankees, getting to the point this way is an admirable trait. To Texans, it's just pushy. A woman who called a Dallas radio show to say her daughter waited on actor Matthew Perry in a local restaurant, complained that the actor was rude. His objectionable behavior? The woman's daughter sat him in the middle of the room, and he told her he wanted a corner booth to be less conspicuous. And one southern friend told me about a blunt critique she received from a colleague on a job. "I was really angry," she said. "Although I would have felt differently if he were a Yankee. Then I would have figured it was just his way."

Of course, Yankee bluntness does have its benefits. When the going gets tough, Yankees rise to the occasion. "Today a group of us went to a sushi bar for lunch," says Ellen. "It was unusually crowded, and a couple of guys bogarted in front of us. I said '*Excuse* me!' I was with a guy from Brooklyn and two Texas gals, who said, 'Let's let Ellen and Michael handle this.'"

But in other situations, Yankee bluntness is a liability. "I was admonished and reprimanded and all kinds of things for being too abrupt at work," says Pat from Massachusetts. "I want to go to a meeting and take care of business. But I learned that first you have to talk: 'So did you go huntin', did ya *keeel* anything?' I couldn't care less, but you have to do that, so now I do."

Texans pad all discussions with chitchat, niceties, blandishments, and qualifiers, and they always have time for a friendly digression. Since moving to Texas, I've become much better at tossing out friendly conversation. I'm not smooth yet, but I'm learning how to make neighborly chitchat that sometimes even approximates folksiness. I can yammer about traffic, the heat, the price of lettuce. Most of the time there is no need to be interesting; all that counts is finding a point of connection between you and the other person. And after spending the first part of my life avoiding eye contact on New York City streets, I've now learned how delightful it can be to catch someone's eye and smile and see a face transformed by a reciprocal smile. It's easy and it's fun, and after twenty years in Texas, I'm a friendlier person than I once was. I'm glad of that.

But when the Texas Department of Highways and Public Transportation wanted to put "The Friendship State" on license plates, Texans let loose an outraged howl. One senator said he had never seen such a negative reaction to a state agency decision. The "Friendship State" was considered too wimpy for Texans. Perhaps "The Friendly State" would have been accepted, since it sounds less needy, more like a noncommittal "howdy."

Because until you understand it, Texans' kindness can kill you.

Newcomer Yankee chicks often are buffeted by Texans' friendliness, first imagining they have friends where they don't, then wondering warily why everyone is being so nice. Some caution is necessary if you don't understand the waltz of southern manners.

When she first arrived in Texas, Maggie from Missouri wore Birkenstocks to a sorority rush at UT. "The girls said, 'Hey, I love your shoes,' and 'Aren't you precious?'" Maggie recalls, sounding slightly bewildered. "I thought they meant it."

No, Texas sorority chicks are not a Birkenstocks crowd, and the girls who gushed over Maggie's comfort-over-beauty shoes were doing what Texas girls do: Being "nice" whether they mean it or not. At the moment, it can be soothing. Later, when the flutter of southern fuss subsides, you think back and wonder, "Hmmm...." You could never accuse these girls of being rude, and they would be devastated by such an accusation. But they weren't being genuinely kind, either.

As Texans don't appreciate Yankee directness, Yankee chicks are not wild for Texans' skill with dissimulation. It takes a while for Yankees to discern the difference between genuine friendliness, plain good manners, and forked-tongue kindness. The southern smile is inscrutable. One southern friend tells me that according to unspoken southern etiquette, the less you like someone, the more polite you are to that person. Feelings must be disguised and if the feeling is negative, the camouflage is applied more thickly.

One of the most public displays of a Yankee getting what I call "Texan-ed" was on the TV show *Survivor*, when L.A. Yankee chick Jerri met Texan hunk Colby. Now, I didn't care for Jerri, but I couldn't help but feel for her as she was increasingly dazzled by the handsome and charming Texan. Jerri was giddy about what appeared to her a budding romance. Meanwhile, Colby was rolling his eyes and spewing venom about her to the camera. Of course this was a game of tactics and double-dealing and Colby was playing along, but what was stunning was Jerri's complete inability to tell that Colby was not feeling anything even remotely reciprocal towards her. This kind of train wreck can happen when Yankee literalness meets Texan opacity.

Truthfully, it is very soothing when confronted with some-thing you don't really want to deal with to just smile blandly and say "How nice" and get on with your life. I do that whenever possible these days. And the longer I'm here, the better I am at recognizing that gentle "what a moron you are" smile when it is directed at me. Messages do slip out from behind even the most polite Texan facade, you only have to recognize them. This can hurt, but it also helps avert episodes of Yankee foot-in-mouth disease.

In Maggie's sorority situation, the message behind "Aren't you precious?" was "You poor ragamuffin, who taught you how to dress?" If the person on the other end of the telephone line says, "I'll let you go now," it means "Lemme off the phone." Mary and Kim, a writer and dancer, respectively, say the sleek ladies of their conservative and high-dollar Dallas neighbor-hood frequently coo about how *creative* and *unique* they are. "What that means is 'we don't get the hell what you're about,'" says Mary.

"Bless your heart" expresses sympathy, but not always kindly. Most often it translates into "you poor little idiot," as in "Bless your heart, that's pronounced 'Ma-*hay*-a'"); or into "I'm not as vicious as I sound"—i.e., "She's dumber than a box of rocks and hasn't had a job since she was fired from McDonald's, bless her heart." The phrase "Bless your heart" is supposed to be effective in declawing catty remarks, but of course it's more a red flag. Nothing irritates savvy Yankee chicks more than a "bless your heart" lobbed their way, though there's nothing to be done but smile through it like a Texan. "Precious" is another word with bless-your-heart connotations, although it is sometimes used genuinely. Pianist Van Cliburn called his mother "Little Precious" and meant it in a big way.

Equally unnerving is Texans' way of dealing with anger. That is, they don't, if they can get away with it. "They are soooo nonconfrontational," says Andrea from Oregon.

"In my world, you say things," says Anne. "If it's good, you tell people. If it's bad, you tell people. You just say it. Here, they feel like they have to go around it."

If a Texan says, "I'm not angry," it may mean, "I'm furious but rather than talk about it I'm going to keep smiling and pretend you don't exist." I had a blossoming friendship with a Texan evaporate for reasons that remain unexplained, although I asked. Doubtless I said or did something appalling in my rude Yankee way, and I would have loved to apologize, but my questions and pleas got me nowhere. "Oh no, nothing is the matter," my friend said with a charming Cheshire grin as she faded from my life. In fact, my pressure for an explanation probably exacerbated the situation. Had a similar situation transpired with a Yankee friend, I can say with complete confidence that she would have been happy to tell me, in 25,000 words or more, the exact way and manner in which I was an insufferable pain-in-the-ass. But the Yankee concept of clearing the air is nearly unheard-of in Texas. "I confronted someone I worked with once," says Pat. "It didn't fix anything. She just stopped talking to me."

"I don't want everyone to lay everything out on the table," insists my friend Texan John. "Honestly, I just don't want to hear about it."

Anger especially is too intimate an emotion to go flapping about in public. Texans like the personal to remain private. Perhaps this explains the endless anguish of country music; it's an acceptable way for southerners to bitch and moan. In *Texasville*, Dwayne's tart-tongued and nearly estranged wife, Karla, has a collection of T-shirts bearing sentiments such as "You're the reason our children are ugly," "Insanity is the best revenge," and "Lead me not into temptation, I'll find it myself." She has new shirts made anytime a new thought occurs to her or when she hears a new sentiment she can get behind. Although her marriage is in deep trouble, the closest she and Dwayne get to discussing the problems are through the messages Karla wears across her chest.

Even in less fraught situations, Texans are uncomfortable with passionate discussion—personal or political—that is the lifeblood of much Yankee intercourse. "I come from a very political family," says Ellen from St. Louis and points northeast. "I get incensed about stuff and very angry. When I was growing up, we could have arguments and nobody ever took it personally. But you can't do that here."

Texans find that kind of conversational verve slightly shocking. While they often talk loudly, it's usually an excess of joviality upping the volume. Texans don't like getting all stirred up in conversation and have ways of sidestepping hot-headed debate. "They make a blanket statement and that's where the conversation ends," says Beth from Indiana. When lefty Joyce tries to debate Rush Limbaugh with her righty Texan in-laws, they give her the old "you just don't like it because the truth hurts" line. And what can you say to that but, "Pass the butter, please."

Personal disclosures may be treated as an embarrassing faux pas. Conversation even with my very closest Texan friends rarely ventures into the very personal, unlike in New York where you can hear the sex lives of total strangers just by eavesdropping on the 104 bus. I recently met a Texan living in California who was newly certified as a psychotherapist. Much as she would like to move back home, she was opting to stay on the left coast because she knew business would be better. It's not that Californians actually have more problems than Texans, she said. It's just that they don't mind talking about them. (Texans, of course, would disagree.)

Once, at a large outdoor wedding, I sat down among a group of Austin hippie-types I did not know. They were discussing medicinal herbs and, after listening a few minutes, I volunteered that I had tried St. John's wort, which is used to treat depression, and that it seemed to work. This divulgence was met by an embarrassed silence while everybody's eyes shifted in every direction but towards me. The conversation ended, and everybody wandered off, leaving me there with a big Yankee foot dangling out of my mouth. In New York, comparing notes about your neuroses is as natural as breaking down Sunday's Cowboys game is here. But if Texan acquaintances are in therapy, you'll never know it. In Texas, people trust in God, use a smile as an umbrella, and don't think any good can come of over-analyzing everything.

Texans are not kvetchers and they have little patience with Yankee-style recreational bitching and moaning. "Complaining is an art form. I love to complain," says Kim from New York. But launch into a New York-style rant and Texans will wait with a fixed and tolerant smile until you've finished, then they will change the subject.

Ever notice how Texans will greet you with "You doin' all right?" as an alternative to "How are you?" My theory on this is that "How are you?" invites a genuine answer Texans don't really want to hear. "You doin' all right?" presumes that you are doing all right, and even if you answer no, Texans can sincerely say, "Well, I hope things get better real soon," and manage to both be compassionate and stay out of any sticky stuff.

While I am adapting to Texas ways, I do still miss some things, like recreational complaining. I miss playing "Top This Personal Revelation." I miss being able to say, "Ahhh, yerfullabaloney," with a dismissive wave and not have anyone take offense. And I'd like to say Texas has made me a more polite person and less of a bitcher and moaner, but that's not the case. Old habits die hard. (Witness this book.) But now, I try to do my complaining around other Yankees, who are more likely to enjoy the sport. With Texans, I just smile and say, "I'm great! Are y'all doin' all right today?"

Chapter Nine

From Friendly to Friendship

"It's like Iowa. They're very friendly up front, but then there's that reserve."

—Melanie, Baltimore, eleven
years in Texas

Meeting people in Texas is easy. Join something.

Perhaps as a reaction to the isolation of the early days of Texas, or perhaps it's yet another influence of the church, but Texans are big on joining things: health clubs, churches, singles groups, charitable organizations. When Mary joined a running group that met at the unholy hour of 6 a.m. every Saturday, she expected to see a few dozen people. To her surprise, about two hundred dragged themselves out of bed to run.

When she first moved to Longview from New York City (imagine!) in the early 1980s, Judy found society hard to crack. "You either were connected or you weren't," she says. "Not 'connected' in terms of society, but everyone knew people through their family. They all had history. It was very, very hard for me to make friends." Judy finally found a gang to run with, including a number of other Yankee transplants, when she joined an organization called the Longview Mother's League. "Do you love that?" she says. "We did things like raise money to decorate the town for Christmas."

I belong to a dining club that meets monthly to try new restaurants. I belonged to two writing groups for a while. I met a woman who is now among my closest friends in group therapy, a club with a Yankee flair.

Mary meets a lot of people through her children's school and through her church, although she advises shopping around for a church society that suits you. "Some churches or Sunday school classes tend to be clique-y and already established; others are really looking to add people and will keep you as busy as you could want to be. There are so many choices, I wouldn't waste a minute with a place that was not friendly or comfortable."

Working chicks make friends on the job. I met nearly all my closest friends at my newspaper job. Newspapers are hotbeds of Yankees and likely to harbor open-minded counter-culture thinkers in Texas's conservative climate, which suited me perfectly. I also met a stellar group of people by volunteering at a nonprofit, which turned out to be both intensely time-consuming and deeply gratifying. Like churches, nonprofits have different personalities. Some of the high-profile boards are difficult to crack and require connections. I started as a lowly committee member on a nonprofit that ultimately rewarded me with a position on the board even though I could barely afford a ticket to the group's annual fund raiser and knew no one with enough money to buy an entire table. Whatever your connections or lack of, you will be able to find a good fit for volunteer work with people who suit you. Theaters, libraries, museums, festivals, all use volunteers, and it's one of those things people do here.

In addition, much Texas society is still wide open and accessible, compared to the entrenched blue bloods of older cities. The Texas ethos that says "if you made a buncha money, you're good enough for me" welcomes all who can afford the price for fund raisers and ball gowns. And before you get to the big-time society soirees, there are starter parties, to groom you. "I went to this Jewish Federation brunch," says Maggie. "Here we were, all these young people in our twenties all dressed up, pretending we had money and could fund raise. I couldn't believe I was doing it." But Texans like to make that scene, and it doesn't matter if you can write big checks or not.

It's practice for when you start the business that earns you your first Texas million.

Texans also like to throw parties. When I first moved down and was trolling for friends, I never said no to an invitation, going alone if necessary. I met my husband at a barbecue, again at a bowling party, and kissed him the first time in the parking lot after another party. Texas parties are frequently large and casual. It's hard to feel ill at ease at a barbecue, with sauce on your cheek and a sunburned nose. If you're a nervous partygoer, just bring a six-pack, push into the kitchen where crowds gather (a worldwide phenomenon), and announce "I've got beer!" Unless you've stumbled into a twelve-step meeting, you will be warmly welcomed.

If you don't yet have enough friends to get party invitations, get on mailing lists for party-like events: art openings, fund raisers, museum lectures. Go, go, go. Lots of people will be there, and since Texans tend to be very more-the-merrier and run with posses, if you meet one person at an event, chances are good they will come with strings of others attached. At some point during or after the event someone is very likely to say, "Should we get some dinner/a drink?" and you can be swept along with the party.

No, meeting people is no problem in Texas. By your first week here, if you get out and about, you'll have met dozens. However for some Yankee chicks, making friends—with all that word's nuances—with Texans can be more challenging. Texans are polite and friendly, but they can be inscrutable. "I'd propose that Texans' 'polite lie' is that we're all gonna be friends and everybody's going to get along great but actually they're going to wait and see, while Yankees sort of act like 'I don't make friends with just anybody' until you warm them up," says Mary.

"In the East, we might have done away with politeness, but we're more up-front," says Anne. "Once you get past the surface, there's lots of depth. Texans show a friendly face to the world, but there are boundaries no one but family can get past."

Even a Texan neighbor commented on a difference at our very first meeting, when she learned of my roots. "You know a lot of people don't like New Yorkers because they think they're rude," this Waco native said, "But I find when they become your friend, it's a very solid, lifelong friendship—more so than here, where everyone seems kind of transient."

Is this all true? Partly, I think it is. I theorize that Yankees' sometimes obnoxious up-frontness about who they are and what they think bonds them quickly to the people who are not put off by them. And their willingness (my weary friends might say eagerness) to express and wrangle with anger keeps them bonded. My closest Texan friends are those who either appreciate my big-mouth New York ways or who have stuck through times of conflict until the friendship came out the other side with new depth. Like the Cheshire cat Texas friend who drifted away from me, one of my very dearest friends nearly slipped away, too. When I finally wore her down with endless nudging, she let loose a 90-minute monologue about everything I had ever done to piss her off in eight years of friendship, punctuated with frequent assurances that she wasn't angry. I didn't believe her—she was spittin' mad and justifiably so. It wasn't fun to hear all my shortcomings, but we remain close friends to this day, even surviving a few spats since then. I believe fights are good for friendship. My Yankee friends are used to that, and my friendships back there were big on heart-to-heart talks, not all initiated by me.

But when I try to get heart-to-hearty here, Texans often back away slowly. When I'm angry and try to explain that I only bother fighting with people I care about, they look profoundly baffled. One friend did finally bear down and open up about some things she needed to say to me. When she was done, she said, "Now that I've told you, I have to kill you." Another friend told me of the time her mother came into a room wearing a paper bag on her head. "She said, 'I have to tell you something and this is the only way I can do it,' and then explained that her long-time roommate was actually her long-time companion." Out of the closet, into the paper bag.

Yankees sometimes find themselves bumping up against Texas family values, too. Because many Texans don't drift far from home, they are already nestled cozily in the bosom of family and a wide circle of friends dating back to the womb. Family ties are strong and deep in Texas, and many of my Texas friends stay busy with myriad family obligations. Their first commitment is almost always to family. This is a fine quality in a human being, but it can sometimes leave the Yankee transplant feeling a little left out. "Everyone always has to hurry home to make dinner for their husbands," sighs Pat, who is single.

Generally Texans treat family as they do Texas itself: If there are problems they are unspoken (at least to outsiders; we can't know what is said in the intimacy of family-only), and everything outside pales in comparison. In *Texasville*, Jacy returns home to Thalia without family (she has divorced and lost a child) and so pilfers her old flame Dwayne's family, from wife to grandchildren. They all move in with her, leaving

Dwayne alone, sad, and broke in his big house. A Texan without family is a Texan adrift. A Yankee without family is often just a Yankee with one less thing to bitch and moan about. (Perhaps the closest Yankee counterpart to the big Texas family is the big Italian family, but it has yelling.)

Last Mother's Day I spoke to my dearest friend in New York and enjoyed a quintessentially Noo Yawk kvetch session about our mothers, during which he filled me in on the trauma another friend was having with *her* mother. After I got off the phone with Monte, I spoke to a close Texas friend who was resting up and basking in the afterglow of a Mother's Day that included celebrations at her mother's house, two of her sisters' houses, and her boyfriend's mother's house. This woman's family Christmas celebrations are so large, they have to rent a hall and draw names for gift giving. Her very dearest friend in the entire world is her niece, who is only slightly younger than she. And for some incomprehensible reason, no matter how many family get-togethers my Texan friends attend, they never seem to come back from them in the state of high anxiety and total regression that I have long considered the hallmarks of family affairs. I am envious and astonished by this.

Fortunately, Texans are generous with their families. I have never once passed a holiday in Texas without being invited to at least one family get-together where I am warmly welcomed, well fed, and invited to come back anytime. I understand, then, why my Texan friends look at me with blank incomprehension when I joke about my own family or, much worse, have the exceedingly poor manners to joke about theirs. (Yes, yes, I am mortified to confess that I have made such an ugly faux pas, not understanding that my Texan friends would not laugh and join in as my New York friends would. There is no

Texas equivalent to the Jewish-mother-guilt joke. In Texas, momma is never a laughing matter.)

So, does that mean friendship across the Mason-Dixon line is impossible? Of course not. When you do push from friendly to friendship with Texans, you'll find them delightful friends (provided, of course, you have good taste in human beings to begin with). They are hospitable, reliable, warm, and upbeat. They come through when you need them. They're generous. I have a standing invitation to use the guest room of one Austin friend's home when none of his family or bajillion other friends are in it, and another friend never visits without bringing me a little gift. (If she's keeping count, and I'm sure she isn't, I probably owe her a Cadillac by now.) Texans are nice to your family. At my wedding, which was in Texas, my parents were pleasantly astonished by how many of my friends spontaneously came up to introduce themselves and make friendly chitchat. Texans, with their polite smiles, can stop you in the middle of a rant that is spiraling out of control (and perhaps if we didn't indulge our rants so much, Yankees wouldn't be so neurotic). And Texans even sometimes grow to appreciate the fact that they can complain to you about stuff and you won't think less of them.

Pray and Tell: Church

In Texas, church is far weightier than just the ethereal matter of personal faith.

I took a philosophy class at a local college. The professor was intelligent, a gifted teacher, a Texan, and, he told me privately, an atheist. He dedicated his career to a small community college, teaching people reared in what has long been practically a Christian monoculture. In his classes, he talked about the tooth fairy, Santa Claus, staffs turning into snakes. He never specifically discussed his personal beliefs with the class, but it was hard not to get the drift.

A thirty-seven-year-old woman who sat near me was clearly dumbfounded by the things he said. She furrowed her brow, chuckled, and shook her head, both fascinated and irritated by the professor's outrageous suggestions. Finally one day, near the end of the semester, she could bear it no longer. She looked at the professor and asked, incredulously, "Do you even go to church?"

Church is so deeply woven into the fabric of life here, Texans find it unthinkable that anyone could not be churchgoing. "Everyone asks 'What church do you go to?' You feel like such a heathen if you don't," says Lucy who moved from Boston a year ago.

Texas certainly makes church attendance convenient. It's not unusual to see two or three churches on a single block, and many Texans attend on Sundays and on Wednesday nights. In Texas, the question is not "do you go to church?" but "*where do you go to church?*" Church is yet another badge of identification, along with car, job, and neighborhood in which you live. In Dallas, if you go to Highland Park United Methodist, you are telling people who you are. This congregation is so packed with power-brokers, it doesn't publish a member directory for fear people would join the congregation just to get this phone book to influence. If you attend Cathedral of Hope, you're either outing yourself or flashing your liberal card, because Cathedral of Hope is the world's largest gay and lesbian congregation. If you worship at St. Luke Community United Methodist Church—a.k.a. "The Church of What's Happening Now"—you're probably among the movers and shakers of Dallas' African-American community. At Cathedral Santuario de Guadalupe, chances are you're among the elite Hispanics.

Entire social lives in Texas are built around church activity, from Bible study to soup kitchens. You can even lose weight the Christian way. First Place, a now-international Christian weight loss program, started at the First Baptist Church in Houston. "You would never see anything like that come out of the churches in the North," says Mary. "Here, church is seen as a place to go to improve yourself for the glory of God. Up North, church is a place to go humble yourself and perhaps wallow in liberal guilt."

Any liberal guilt you may harbor can also be assuaged in church. Church activity is a powerful force in charity in Texas, filling the gap between need and state spending on social services. If you ever find yourself homeless or otherwise downtrodden, look for the nearest church. You might not always agree with the causes churches get behind, but you can't help but be awed by their ability to mobilize and get things done. If a church gets involved, things happen.

The enthusiasm Texans have for their church makes them anxious to share the life with everyone. Texans want you to be like them, which can be trying if you're not. I once found myself stopped behind a car with a bumper sticker reading, "If you haven't accepted Christ as your personal savior, you are going to HELL" the last word engulfed in flames.

That kind of thing makes a lot of Christians wince, but even perfectly nice people don't always think things through. The friendly man at the post office never looked me in the eye again after I politely requested nonreligious stamps instead of Virgin Mary stamps. A friend from Oklahoma didn't realize that "jewed him down" had a meaning beyond haggling. Anne, who works at a newspaper, talked an editor out of running the headline, "Jewish facility christened." Few people intend to be mean, but some suffer from an excess of conviction or never thought of it "that way."

In Texas, the moment you move into a new house, neighbors appear to welcome you to their congregation. They invite you to Bible study, leave church fliers in your mailbox, and generally try to sell you on their way of life. Church here is imbued with the same entrepreneurial spirit that makes the state a great place to do business. "I'm a top producer for God and a broker-Realtor," said one woman in a

Dallas Morning News article about a 13,000-member, $46 million megachurch in Plano. She claimed to bring 150 people to the church each year and testify to three to five people daily. Other members of her congregation left waiters tracts along with tips, urged their children to testify to friends, and proselytized to shop clerks. "If you see them getting annoyed, you know God hasn't softened their heart yet," said the top producer for God. "You back off, and you pray for them." If I get backed into a corner by this kind of overenthusiastic savior, I just tell myself it's all done with the best of intentions by people who are only worried because I am going to burn in HELL!

Of course, as Texas changes, other religions are raising their own voices, too. I receive an amazing number of mailings, sometimes several daily, from Jewish institutions in Dallas. The power of the church encompasses all religions in Texas, and while the Christian church is the Big Kahuna here, all institutions of worship bask in the power it bestows on organized religion.

If you have any inclination towards church at all, there's a good chance you'll slip into the habit, since it is so wholeheartedly encouraged, and you'll have an awful lot of churches to choose from. After twelve years of looking, Joyce has found a "progressive church that comes pretty close to my spiritual beliefs." Dana found an ethnically and economically mixed Catholic church where she is comfortable. Melanie found an interdenominational and interracial church she likes. "It's huge," she says.

"You have to get there at 8 a.m. to get a parking spot for the 10 a.m. service. It was like back East, in that you had the black women with the huge hats, but it had more of the white worship style. Less Holy Roller and more Praise worship."

Preachers here might sound peculiar to Yankee ears, "Our minister is pretty reasonable, theologically, and well educated, but he sounds like an old-time preacher—very 'country,'" Mary, a Methodist, says. "I think southerners equate that style with theological purity; while northerners associate it with ignorance and a kind of backwoods fanaticism. We had a more literate, lofty-sounding guy before, and a lot of the congregation thought he was a pointy-headed equivocating pansy. Which he was, a little bit, but he'd be able to get away with it up north."

Non-churchy Yankee chicks can just say "thanks but no thanks" to church and Bible study invitations. Most people will back off quickly. In addition, when in doubt, assume everyone around you is churchgoing and behave accordingly. In fact, you might as well assume everyone is Christian until you learn otherwise. One woman I know seemed Jewish as my Aunt Tilly (with a different accent), right up until the moment when she invited me to her church. ❧

Chapter Ten

As a Matter of Fact, I Do Own the Road

"I commuted ten years on the Long Island Expressway in the weekend traffic and never had a wreck. I had two in my first year in Dallas."

—Kim, New York, three years in Texas

*A*ll the hostility Texans keep pent up by being unfailingly polite face-to-face is unleashed on the highways. Texans drive fast, they drive aggressively, and they don't give an inch or a damn.

Let's mince no words.

"I hate the drivers here," says Judy from New York.

Me too. I used to like them—their glamorous fearlessness, their cocky confidence. But as Texas has become considerably more crowded in past decades, fearless has become foolish. Or, as I put it in my charming Yankee way every time I see a fender bender or worse: "Someone was probably driving like a f*** a****." Nothing puts the sewer in my mouth like aggressive Texas driving.

In Texas, a merge is not a traffic pattern, but a power struggle. A merge sign, for the driver entering the highway, is a signal to jam the accelerator and beat the oncoming traffic. For the driver on the highway, the sight of someone trying to merge is a signal to jam the accelerator so that S.O.B. doesn't get ahead. It's a game of chicken played with squinty sidelong glances at each other until one of two things happens: One driver either decides that highway humiliation is preferable to death in a flaming wreck and slows down; or he decides that death is preferable to dishonor and increases to time-warp speed, pulling ahead with a roar. For extra fun in this scenario, watch the faces of passengers in the competitive cars. With nothing at stake but their lives, they can afford to look terrified.

The same get-offa-my-road attitude holds true for lane changes. Texans rarely signal lane changes because the blinking light is code for other drivers to speed up and fill in any gaps that might allow someone to get ahead. To change lanes, you have to slip in kamikaze, catch other drivers off-guard.

And while I wouldn't say Texans are the fastest drivers in the country (Massachusetts drivers are strong contenders), they do keep a brisk pace. On a drive to East Texas one Saturday morning, I set my cruise control to the speed limit, which was a healthy 75. I might as well have been poking along at 70. Cars blasted by going 80, 85. There is no such thing as fast enough here. There are two speed limits in Texas. The one on the sign, and five miles over that, which is considered the *real* speed limit. If the sign read 100 mph, Texas drivers would consider 105 mph the speed limit. Speeders would drive faster.

Personally, I've opted out of the race. I used to speed, now I am one of approximately seven drivers in Texas who does not. It's my own private protest, and it annoys the hell out of other drivers and a lot of my passengers, too. Drivers glare at me as they zoom past, blowing raspberries of exhaust. I don't drive dangerously slow, just the speed limit, which is slow enough to require most drivers to pass me. And while I used to stay politely in the right lane, where slowpokes belong by law, I've now moved into the middle, since the right has become just another passing lane. As a courtesy, I give drivers a choice of lanes, to my right or left, in which to pass. I once heard a radio caller complain that people driving the speed limit don't belong in the right lane because we obstruct people entering and exiting the highway. But his solution was different from mine. He insisted we don't belong on the highway at all, that anyone who wants to drive the speed limit should be confined to the access road.

It did not surprise me to learn that in 2001, three of the nation's five most dangerous intersections were in the Dallas area. And Texans are becoming habitual red light runners. For this problem Texas congressman Dick Armey recommended the solution of making yellow lights longer. Texans staunchly defend their right to drive like lunatics. Even parking lots can be terrifying because of all the people who seem to believe that laws of physics are suspended once you leave the street. In parking lots, cars can come hurtling at you from any direction as they cut across rows and lanes in any way that is expedient. It's the Texas way.

Texans go into a major dither in winter storms. Yankees laugh at Texans who refuse to get out on icy roads, but they don't laugh long. Driving on Texas ice is different from driving on Yankee snow. First of all, Texas's warm days cause ice on roads to melt slightly. When the sun goes down, the melted ice refreezes into a lethal sheet. Add the death wish of Texas-style driving, and you have good reason to stay home on ice days. Maybe you know how to drive in inclement weather, but do you want to be in the intersection when Joe Bob in his pickup, barreling towards the yellow light at 60 mph, hits a piece of black ice?

Texans drive this way because it's the cool thing to do. As the car you drive makes a statement, so does the way you drive. One-armed driving, a guy thing, is cocky and a little dangerous, developed so the other arm could hold either a girl or a beer. If you're fortunate enough to have both, your beer nestles between your legs. This is slowly changing as lax open-container laws have toughened up. When I arrived, driving drunk was illegal but driving drinking was not. It wasn't unusual to see a pickup truck bed piled with beer cans, tossed back there from the cab with an insouciant gesture. First a law was passed prohibiting drivers from drinking, although passengers could.

In 2001 a law prohibiting any open container of alcohol in the car was passed.

My friend Texan John is a one-arm wrist driver. The control of the car is entirely held by his one meaty wrist resting on the steering wheel. Tom and I went to Italy with John and his wife, and he did the one-arm wrist driving thing at 70 mph in the left lane on Italy's highways while Tom and I clutched each other white-knuckled in the back seat. Of course, when I drove, I could hear John and Helen's thought balloons join with one thought: "We're never going to get there at this rate." John laughs at my fear and points out that Helen's rule is that he always has to have at least one hand on the wheel, since he also drives with his knees sometimes.

Other driving styles include what I've heard called the Detroit Lean (apparently a Yankee import), seen mostly in young black men who tilt their seats back and list heavily to the right as they one-arm drive with their left hands. Lowriders in low-riders sit back in their plushy upholstery and drive slooooow, so you have time to admire their handiwork. At stoplights, they rev up the hydraulics, shimmying, bouncing, and bowing. Businessmen, phones pressed to their ears, weave through traffic with nervous type-A glances around them, everything about their demeanor saying they have important things to do, places to go, deals to cut. Drivers of pickups take particular liberties since they hold the power not only of vehicle size, but mystique. Don't argue with a pickup truck, especially if you're at the wheel of a wimpy Yankee car. The elderly, in big yellow Cadillacs or sun-bleached vintage pickups, grip the wheel with both hands and look straight ahead, setting their own pace, letting traffic dart around them, daring anyone to try to take away their lifeline to independence.

Road Hints

Learning your way around Texas cities can be challenging. There's no shame in keeping a MAPSCO book of maps handy, everyone does. A MAPSCO number often accompanies written directions. If it weren't for MAPSCO, I probably would have gotten hopelessly lost within my first three hours in Texas and would still be driving around in circles, trying to find my way out of Mesquite. (For some reason whenever I get lost, I end up in Mesquite, a Dallas suburb. Except the time I took a series of wrong turns out of downtown Dallas and ended up 20 miles out of my way, in Grapevine.)

Particularly confusing to newcomers is the way Texans use local designations and highway numbers interchangeably. In Dallas, you have to know that LBJ and 635 are the same highway, as are Stemmons and 35, Central and 75. In Austin, the MOPAC (named for the Missouri and Pacific Railroad, that used to follow that route) is also 1. Hint: Access road signs often have the local names while highway signs have numerical designation. In Houston, and seemingly no place else, "access roads" or "frontage roads" are called "feeder streets."

Some streets change names in different parts of town. In Dallas, Loop 12 morphs into Northwest Highway, Walton Walker Boulevard, Ledbetter Drive, and probably other names I haven't yet encountered. Nobody knows the city completely. Never be too proud to ask for detailed directions. You don't want to be a dawdling, confused driver, annoying the locals.

Driving in the boonies is considerably more restful. It's not much slower, unless you get caught behind a tractor on a two-lane highway in which case, relax and look at the pretty scenery. But it is friendlier. In West Texas, it's traditional to give a little index-finger wave to oncoming drivers. On two-lane country roads, I always pull to the right to let speedy drivers pass. I may be there to admire the scenery, but if they're locals, chances are good they spend a lot of time driving from place to place. I don't want to mess with their day. In the Hill Country, keep your eyes open for sudden clots of cars by the side of the road, often a telltale sign of a swimming hole. ❧

Texans are libertarians on the road, believing in their right to do whatever they can get away with without killing anyone. However, Texans are not casual honkers. Horns are used even less frequently than turn signals. A gentle toot is OK if someone is asleep at the wheel when the light turns green, and Texans are not averse to an angry *BLAAAAAAAAT* if you cut them off, intentionally or not, whether they come up behind you at a searing 95 mph or a sedate 70. But even in the most dense traffic, you'll never hear the cacophony of horns you hear on New York streets.

Yet for all the horror of Texas city streets and highways, I'm not giving up my wheels anytime soon. I lived without a car my first six months in Dallas, and it was a monumental hassle. You have to weasel a lot of rides if you want to have any kind of life at all. The first time I ever took a bus in Dallas was to a job interview. I arrived without incident but afterwards, unclear on how public transportation (such as it was) operated, I simply walked to a bus stop and waited. After nearly an hour, during which I turned down a number of men offering me lifts, a policeman finally stopped and asked what I was doing. He then explained that a) because it wasn't rush hour the bus wasn't scheduled to arrive for hours and b) nice girls don't stand around on this particular street. What did I know? It doesn't look anything like 9th Avenue, where working girls work it in Manhattan, so I figured it was OK. I called a roommate to rescue me.

Public transportation has vastly improved in Dallas since then but does not yet lend itself to winging it. It doesn't run all night and it can't get you anywhere you want to go in a timely manner. And Dallas actually has a pretty sophisticated public transportation system compared to other Texas cities. Houston has a bus system that works for downtown commuters and few others. San Antonio has nothing to speak of. Austin grew too fast to even think about it yet.

Since joining the car culture, I've given up what I used to call my "New York purse"—a huge tote in which I could carry everything from a change of shoes to a novel for the subway. Now I use my car as a sort of purse-on-wheels instead. I carry a lot of crap in my car: piles of aging junk mail I've picked up from the post office; plastic bags to drop in the recycling bin at the supermarket if I ever remember; an empty plastic water bottle that I could reuse someday; an old French fry I'm saving for later. The exterior of my car wears layers of shmutz for much longer than is considered proper.

That's my Yankee showing. Texans keep their cars clean. The first sunny day after rain, car washes are jammed. You rarely see a really filthy car in Dallas, other than mine.

This is one of the signals I send out to the world. Nothing says "Yankee" like a dirty seven-year-old Honda driving the speed limit.

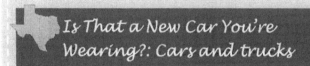

Is That a New Car You're Wearing?: Cars and trucks

In Texas, your car is your ultimate accessory. You put on underwear, clothes, and car, in that order. Your car is your trademark, an extension of your identity. By the second paragraph of McMurtry's quintessentially Texas novel *The Last Picture Show*, he has already introduced us to two cars: the night watchman Andy Fanner's Nash and Sonny's '41 Chevrolet pickup. No character in the book is without distinguishing wheels. Teen queen Jacy drives a white Ford convertible; her mother, rich, bored Lois, drives a Cadillac; dejected Mrs. Popper drives a '53 Chevy; rich and dissolute Bobby Sheen drives the "first Ford Thunderbird in that part of the country." When Bible-thumping Joe Bob takes off on a pathetic sexual misadventure, it's in the family Plymouth; and repressed homosexual Coach Popper celebrates the success of a dastardly plan to out a fellow teacher with a shiny red V8—car as phallus. And in *Dwayne's Depressed*, the third book in the trilogy that started with *The Last Picture Show*, Dwayne decides that too much of his life has passed by while he was driving around in a pickup truck and decides to walk everywhere. The town decides he's insane.

When you visit people in Texas, they peek out the window not for a glimpse of you, but of the car that represents you. I remember vividly the sight of my now-husband pulling up in front of my apartment in his little Nissan pickup for our first date. Tom is from Chicago and his was a Yankee/Texan car—a Japanese pickup. He now drives a Ford pickup, the truck favored by urban cowboys. Real cowboys drive Chevys.

Your car makes your statement to the world. What possible reason could there be to buy a Lincoln Continental SUV except to show you can? Pickup trucks posture aggressively up and down the highways, spittin' tobacco on piss-ant Hondas. Sexy little Mercedes convertibles purr along, driven by middle-aged men, their comb-overs flapping merrily in the breeze. College students pile into Jeeps with roll bars, car as amusement park ride. Secretaries tool along in serviceable little domestic cars with hopeful names like Breeze and Aspire. Hispanic men strut through town in elaborate, pampered lowriders while their families pile into conversion vans, the SUV of the lower-middle class. Gleaming new SUVs barrel through traffic, kids in the back, mom with cell phone pressed to her ear (soccer moms are the nation's common denominator).

On a popular Dallas radio show, the morning crew discussed the resume of a new intern, who had held all sorts of saintly positions, helping the downtrodden and making the world a better place. "But didn't she have some kind of really cool job?" one of the crew asked. "Oh yeah," said the other. "She drove the Zamboni at the Galleria skating rink."

I once had a car stolen right from the driveway of the fourplex I lived in. The policeman's eyebrows shot up when I told him what sort of car it was. "Who would steal a Rabbit?" he asked. Surprisingly (or perhaps not), the car was found. It was fine, except the radio had been changed to an easy-listening station. Apparently, in Texas, Rabbits are stolen by wimpy car thieves who like Olivia Newton-John.

The love affair with wheels probably started as an extension of the cowboy's love affair with his horse. One man, one horse, except that one horse, with just one horsepower, isn't the best way to cover a state the size of Texas. So the traditional cowboy eventually kissed his horse goodbye and drove into the sunset in a pickup. Suddenly, a ranch that once took days to cover could be toured in hours. The massive state was rendered accessible, given some time and a full tank of gas or twelve. Pickup trucks remain the vehicle of choice, whether or not you have anything to haul. By driving a pickup, the Texan stays connected to the vehicle as beast of burden, to the days when he might need to carry a few bales of hay. Now pickup trucks mostly carry lawn mowers and friends' furniture when they move (the guy with the pickup is always the first person called after the lease is signed), but Texas remains the No. 1 market for pickups in the country, which is the No. 1 market for pickup trucks in the world. Nothing says Texan like a pickup.

The Texan-car bond solidified with the oil boom, when every gas-guzzlin', honkin'-big statusmobile on the road was putting money in some good ol' boy's pocket. The Rolls Royce dealership in oil-rich Midland was recognized for being one of the top three dealers in the United States. How could you not love cars? They represented freedom and wealth. Cars were good to Texans, Texans are good to their cars. Riding around in a car became and remains something to do in Texas, both out of necessity and for the fun of it. Much of *The Last Picture Show* and *Texasville* occurs in cars. In her memoir, Barbara Jordan recalled being thrilled that her roommate at Boston College had a brand-new black Ford convertible, disappointed that the roommate wasn't interested in riding around in it, "like I was used to." Signs around the city advising that turns cannot be made during certain evening hours are to discourage cruising, certainly not a Texas phenomenon but enthusiastically embraced here.

Texans were devastated by the oil bust not only in economic terms. It hurt their feelings, too. I lived in Texas during that time, and although I counted no millionaire oilmen in my social circle, I recall the feeling of the bottom dropping out of the excited Urban Cowboy buzz. A lot of Yankees went home, and Texas, a little stunned, a little sadder, a lot wiser, shook it off, regrouped, and diversified. Texas relies less on oil these days, but oil retains a place alongside the Alamo and cowboys in the Texas mystique. When gas prices go up (though they are still a fraction of prices in other countries) the news media rush out to gas stations to interview people filling their big vehicles. Texans just shrug and say, "Well that's what it takes," and pull out their credit cards. Sometimes they mutter darkly about conspiracies. But it's the rare Texan who says, "I'm tired of being a gas hog; I'm trading in my Explorer." The right to drive a big car is sacrosanct here. As Dick Cheney said in defense of drilling in the Alaskan wilderness, "the American way of life is blessed." To which Texans say "Amen." ✦

Chapter Eleven

The Look

"*I had to get 300 stitches after my car accident. The plastic surgeon who sewed my face up kept trying to sell me on all this other stuff. Finally, he said, 'Let me just say two words: breast enhancement.'*"

—Kim, New York, three years in Texas

I was in Dallas one early autumn, job-hunting before I moved down. As I crossed a large office-building lobby, nervously en route to an interview, I scarcely noticed a woman coming towards me. But then, as we passed each other, she leaned over and whispered in my ear, *"It's too early for boots."*

When Linda arrived in Texas, she answered an employment ad for a personal assistant. "I got all dressed up, in my way," she says. "I think my dress was from Pier One." At the employment agency, she took typing and spelling tests, performing well on the former and perfectly on the latter. But then, after her interview, the man who did the interviewing proceeded to tell her about the previous applicant, who came impeccably dressed in suit and cleavage. "And as a man," he said, "How could I not notice?" He then advised Linda, "You don't have the flash to make it in Dallas," and ended the interview.

You will be graded.

Texas women always look great. Whether they're modish as a Dallas chick at Neiman Marcus; over-the-top Texan, with big hair and sparkly, jangly clothes; or in kicker-chic skintight Rocky Mountain jeans, you know they put thought, effort, and considerable time into their appearance. Clothing and grooming are central to the cult of the Texas woman. Texas women shine. They glisten. They gleam. Every one of them has it and knows how to use it, or at the very least where she can get it.

In *Deep in the Heart of Texas* former Dallas Cowboys cheerleader Stephanie Scholz writes, "...fooling a man is easier than convincing a four-year-old about Santa. A one-hundred-dollar dye job, a couple thousand dollars' worth of makeup at your vanity, and weekly worship services at Neiman's. And, sweetheart, it's like ringing the dinner bell at Pavlov's house."

OK, Stephanie is over the top. So was Robert Altman in *Dr. T. and the Women*, in which the women all sashay around Dallas' Northpark Mall in leopard prints, trailing furs, candy-colored suits, and gigantic hat concoctions. The images are absurd and overblown, but they carry a nugget of truth. "I'll never forget the shock of going to Northpark the very first time and realizing I was underdressed," says Melanie from Delaware.

"Even relaxed Texas women are more turned out than me," says Anne. "I went to hear a band at a club the other night, and whereas on the East Coast it would be jeans and T-shirts, here it was short skirts and tall strappy sandals."

Texas chicks are outfitty. Top, bottoms, shoes, accessories—nothing looks thrown together. This style crescendos at the holiday season, when they festoon themselves merrily with Christmas sweaters, angel earrings, candy-striped socks, and precious little baby Taylor in a matching outfit, her big red bow askew on her bald head.

The Christmas sweater phenomenon has long fascinated me. Christmas sweaters are sometimes quite elaborate (a critical person might say garish) with gifts and baubles and candy canes and whatnot hanging off them, and they are often quite expensive. Yet they are the uniform of Christmas shopping. I'm still not clear if women wear the same Christmas sweater for the entire holiday season or if they have wardrobes of Christmas sweaters, entire storage rooms of Christmas sweaters, to keep them suitably festooned throughout the holiday season. Do you have to get a new Christmas sweater every year? Can

Christmas sweater aficionados tell when you're wearing last year's model? At what point do you have to tuck your Christmas sweaters away until next year? People leave their Christmas lights up for months after the fact. Can you get away with wearing a Christmas sweater in, say, mid-February, when you might need a little Christmas? Nowadays, Thanksgiving sweaters and Halloween sweaters are also staples of the ever-lengthening holiday season.

While Dallas tops the list of grooming-conscious cities in the state (if not the country or the world) all Texas women take their grooming seriously. In Austin, you nurture a style that suits your SUV with the canoe strapped on top. In San Antonio, you doll up in sassy Western wear. In gala-happy Houston, dressing for social events is a serious job. "I went to a cancer society gala and it was an exhausting all-day thing getting ready for it," says Pat. "You couldn't just throw a little black dress on. You had to get a gown and the whole bit. Down here, you have to have the matching shoes."

Attention to detail is bred into women all over the state, and while women in the country might not pore over *Vogue* like city chicks, they have their standards. "When Toni home permanents came out, that was a great breakthrough. Mama said no self-respecting woman would have straight hair once they'd invented Toni home permanents," wrote Ann Richards, who grew up in a small town outside Waco. Richards has, of course, taken her mama's word to heart in grand fashion. When she turned sixty, her big Austin bash included cotton candy spun in the shape of her trademark coif.

"While critics argue that a woman's appearance is only superficial, I disagree," wrote the late cosmetic millionaire Mary Kay Ash in *You Can Have It All*. "When a woman changes from an ugly duckling into a beautiful swan, something inside changes, too. Outer beauty kindles inner beauty."

But that outer beauty can be a beast to develop.

Being a chick is time-consuming in Texas, requiring much shopping, hairdoing, exfoliating, spritzing, spraying, powdering, scenting, and manicuring. If men prove their manhood with the thrill of football, women prove themselves with the agony of the bikini wax. It takes steely determination and a lot of time to keep up with the most dedicated Texas chicks, but chances are you will be sucked into the whole grooming obsession to some extent. "I went to a wedding in Connecticut and realized how much I had really changed," says Pat. "Everybody else had the little navy dress with the pearls. I wore cubic zirconium earrings, red lipstick, bright coral dress, lots of hairspray, more jewelry than everybody else. I stood out."

Dana says, "I was walking out the door today, and I thought, I can't believe I'm going out without a manicure. I never would have cared in New York. I didn't get manicures, and I'd be talking with my hands anyway. But now I'm hiding my hands; I don't want anyone to see."

I moved to Texas with a carefully collected wardrobe of vintage clothing. It didn't take long to realize that in my job at an advertising agency, the "vintage" clothes that defined my style in New York were actually merely old and ratty. I went shopping immediately. I recall one very blonde, very Texas account executive at this same agency returning from her first trip to New York thoroughly unimpressed. "I've always heard about how stylish the women of New York are, but I don't think they looked good at all," she said, wrinkling her nose. "I saw women on the street wearing tennis shoes with their suits."

Karen left Los Angeles an alabaster-skinned, raven-haired, black-clad Goth chick. "When I first moved down, I wore all black to a beer bar, and I could tell I was a freak on wheels," she says. "Here, I didn't know anyone who dyed her hair black. In L.A., tons of people do. It's not like the whole city was Gothic or anything, but at least there were others. I moved to Texas and realized nobody's going to be impressed with the way I looked. They appreciated my efforts, but nobody cared if I didn't try that hard." In ten years in Texas, Karen's hair color has softened, her skin is not as white, her wardrobe is less funereal. "Now, instead of a sea of black, I've had to get other colors. You can't wear black in the summer, it's too hot. Gothic would never have been invented here."

I shop more carefully than I ever did before and I've surprised myself on occasion by matching top to bottom or purse to shoes. My style has not been entirely eclipsed—I still don't own a single pair of tall strappy sandals—but I've gotten addicted to things like facials and having my brows professionally shaped. And I've been sucked deeper and deeper into the world of hair product. Classic big hair is not quite the player it was in the 1980s, although it is still out there and you'll have some breathtaking sightings now and then. However, everyone's hair seems to get a little bit bigger in Texas. Many of us experience a sort of gravitational pull towards, at the very least, mousse and hairspray. Flat hair is unthinkable unless it's pulled back into a fetching casual ponytail, perhaps peeking saucily from the back of a baseball cap. I now judge the success of my hair by volume: Is it bigger than my head? If not, I wear a cap.

However, I have not succumbed to blonde and never will. That's too Texas for my blood.

"I think it is quite possible to grow up in Texas an utter failure in flirting, gentility, cheerleading, sexpottery, and manipulation and still be without permanent scars. Except one. We'd all rather be blonde," Molly Ivins wrote. Against all genetic odds, in the movie *Giant*, even raven-haired Rock Hudson and Elizabeth Taylor manage to crank out a couple of blonde children. Otherwise, no one would have believed they were born in Texas. When upscale department store Barneys New York opened in Dallas in the 1990s, word got out that stylists at the in-store salon were dissing the blondeness that is Dallas, suggesting stylists were steering clients to the wrong bottle. The city was outraged. Of course, it was the damn Yankees again. "People tell me they just feel uncomfortable there because they're from New York and they want you to feel uncomfortable,'" groused the assistant manager of a competitive salon. Barneys is long gone but blondeness lives on, the result of equal parts German ancestors and modern chemicals.

Texas African-American chicks are less likely to go blonde (it has been known to happen), but they do have their own version of hair obsession. Some sport some of the most complicated hairstyles I've ever seen, with twists and marcels and frizzes and blonde tips and pin curls, sometimes all at once, in museum-worthy flights of creativity. The majority if these 'dos have one thing in common: processed hair. Afro chicks who don't want to go for chemicals have had to conquer stigma (two police officers—one male, one female—were fired from the Dallas police force for refusing to cut their dreadlocks), but that is changing as Texas changes. "With all the people coming from other places now, I'm starting to feel more comfortable not being the pressed-haired buttoned up black chick that I was when I first got here," says Melanie, who has let her hair go natural and joined a support group of other women who have made the same decision. "I haven't straightened my hair in decades, says Linda from Detroit, founder of that support group, A Happy Nappy Hair Affair. "I had several friends who complained about not being able to find anyone to help with their natural hair, who understood their hair and gave it the same concern and attention they gave perms."

Perms, dye jobs, boob jobs. Like in Hollywood, in Texas all is OK in the name of looking sensational. In Texas, looking good on the outside counts in all you do, from hair to home. Judy, a realtor, says, "It never ceases to amaze me how important 'drive-up appeal' is here. Again and again folks give up practical considerations for gorgeous, cute, charming or pay an enormous premium for it." It's all part of the same mind set.

According to a 2000 article in the *Houston Chronicle*, Texas ranks first in the nation in fat injections to smooth wrinkles or make lips pouty; second in the number of butt-lifts and breast implant removals; third in face-lifts, thigh lifts, and chemical peels; and fourth in boob jobs, liposuction, and the number of certified plastic surgeons. (California is the leader in most categories, with Florida, Texas, and New York following closely.) A wrinkle cream manufacturer tells us that Texans spend 21.1 minutes on their facial appearance each day, more than any other state in the nation, where the average is 15 minutes. A rep for a brassiere company once told me he sells more 32D bras in Dallas than anywhere else. (Think about it: That particular size combination doesn't happen often in nature.) And heed this cautionary take: One woman I know, who prided herself on *always* being able to spot a boob job made a snippy comment about someone's boob job to another woman. "Um," said the woman. "You know, I've had mine done...." You never know who's packin' these days so make no assumptions. Boobs are highly coveted and easy to get. And don't be shocked if a newly boobed friend gleefully lifts her shirt to show you the great job her doc did. It's been known to happen. Like everything else in Texas, if you want something, you work hard, earn lots of money, buy it, and show it off.

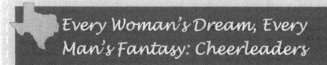

Every Woman's Dream, Every Man's Fantasy: Cheerleaders

I've been to one Dallas Cowboys game and spent the entire time mesmerized by the Dallas Cowboys Cheerleaders' hair. I'd never seen such hair before. They could flip it and toss it and swirl it and it never mussed. It shone, it bounced, it looked touchable no matter how much dancing and prancing it was subjected to. And I knew then, in a way I'd never fully understood, that Texas cheerleaders are a different species of woman from me. "The pick of the litter," said Cowboys owner Jerry Jones, and he meant it as a compliment.

Modern cheerleading was developed at Dallas' Southern Methodist University in Dallas by a guy, Lawrence Herkimer, who invented the pom-pom and the Herkie jump, which is that classic jump where one leg kicks forward and the other bends back. He also founded the National Cheerleading Association. But the hometown connection is only a sidebar to the state obsession with cheerleaders. "I was a cheerleader and it was totally different. It was just something you did. It wasn't a lifestyle," says Melanie from Baltimore.

The Cult of the Cheerleader is sister to the Church of Football in Texas. Cheerleaders are the virgin brides of the game's gladiators, nuns to football players' priests. Though they carry none of the power of the church, cheerleaders do have a place in the Friday night service.

That men like cheerleaders is not hard to figure out. That girls and women clamor to be cheerleaders is a little murkier, aside from the opportunity to be "every man's dream woman, every woman's dream come true," as Mary Candace Evans writes breathlessly in *A Decade of Dreams*, an official Dallas Cowboys Cheerleaders history.

"The intoxicating applause and the clamor wherever we went...were not our only motivations," wrote former Dallas Cowboys Cheerleader Stephanie Scholz in her memoir *Deep in the Heart of Texas*. "It was the fact that we'd all been brought up to believe in everything that the Dallas Cowboys Cheerleaders stood for—the institution of football and cheerleading. When I pranced out on the field I was fulfilling my childhood dreams. And 65,000 people were screaming their approval, shouting in deafening emphasis that they shared my dreams." (Can you remember any moment in your life when you could be said to have "pranced"?)

Cheerleader training starts young in Texas, with peewee squads of five- and six-year-olds who can barely spell V-I-C-T-O-R-Y. In 1997 a local football association drew a line when it forbade a peewee squad to use the song "Barbie Girl" in a competition because it included such lyrics as "Undress me everywhere . . . Kiss me here, kiss me there, hanky panky. . . . " By high school, those who continue to make the cut are at the top of the mainstream hierarchy. It's a perilous perch, though. Cheerleaders are held to standards of behavior that seem intended to cancel out the short skirts. When four cheerleaders on a sixteen-member squad at a school outside Houston got pregnant, the girls were booted from the squad and the story made national news. In 1996 another couple of teens were tossed from a squad after being caught smoking.

Molly Ivins wrote, "That Baptists see nothing wrong with the Dallas Cowboys Cheerleaders, who are indisputably open-air coochie girls, is one of those anomalies we all live with here." But by keeping a cloak of apparent chastity on the women of the squad while uncloaking the rest of them, Texas manages to bear up. The Dallas Cowboys Cheerleaders wear hot pants and pose for swimsuit calendars, but may not date players, coaches, or employees of the club or drink or smoke while in uniform. They may not even be photographed with someone holding alcohol. When Jerry Jones bought the Cowboys and threatened not only to allow fraternizing with the players, but also to change the uniform to halter and bike shorts, fourteen cheerleaders resigned in protest fearing, as one cheerleader sniffed, that with such relaxed standards, the Dallas Cowboys Cheerleaders would be degraded to no better than the Miami Dolphins cheerleaders.

The Dallas Cowboys Cheerleaders are quick to stress how much of their time is spent visiting sick children and cheering up troops overseas. And cheerleading does have its own pain. A 1999 study identified cheerleading as one of the most dangerous sports for women, especially since the gymnastic ante at the college level is ever-upping, with flips and tosses and other high-flying stunts. Former Dallas Cowboys general manager Tex Schramm, who created the team's famous cheerleader squad, first tried putting models on the sidelines, but the heat and exertion nearly killed them. The Dallas Cowboys Cheerleaders might not do stunts, but they dance, prance, and toss their hair through entire games, whatever the heat. In addition, they attend 2-5 unpaid rehearsals each week ("CANDIDATES WHO DO NOT FEEL THEY CAN ATTEND ALL REHEARSALS SHOULD NOT CONTEMPLATE BEING A DALLAS COWBOYS CHEERLEADER," the audition literature cautions); maintain their own uniforms (it must be hard to keep white hot pants looking fresh in the heat); and watch their weight. "I'll take the shorts up but I won't let them out," the Dallas Cowboys Cheerleaders costumer cautions the girls. "Cheerleaders gaining weight to an extreme are warned, then put on nonperforming status, and finally terminated from the squad," the rules threaten. All this for $50 per home game (though they are paid for other appearances), and no job security. Everyone must audition every year.

And they if love it anyway, what can we say?

Making fun of cheerleaders is too easy to be fun. It's easy to come up with a hundred feminist reasons to dis the obsession. "Basically, you're teaching girls to stand on the sidelines and cheer men," sighs Melanie. And the emphasis placed on it can be distressing and sometimes downright balmy. I know women well past cheerleader age who still carry faint bruises from not being considered cheerleader material in their school days. In *The Positively True Adventures of the Alleged Texas Cheerleader-Murdering Mom*, Holly Hunter played Wanda Holloway, a Houston woman convicted of solicitation of capital murder for hiring a hit man to bump off the mom of her daughter's rival for a spot on the squad. (Her reasoning was that the girl would be too distraught to give it the old cheerleader oomph.) Recently, one Houston-area school ended up with sixty cheerleaders on its squad, instead of its usual thirty (most schools have twelve) when it was revealed the judging had been rigged. In its own way, cheerleading is as dangerous as football, though more bruising to self-esteem than bodies.

Cheerleading lives in the same gray zone as the Miss America Pageant, which insists it is more scholarship program than beauty pageant. You're delighted the women are getting the money but wish they didn't have to parade around in bathing suits and heels to win it.

Cheering is athletic in its own way, and it can be presented as more than short skirts and big smiles. The mission statement for SMU's spirit squads (the co-ed cheerleader squad and the all-chick pom-pon squad) is "to maximize individual potential through experiences directed toward developing community spirit."

If you think of it that way, it's not so bad, is it? But support the WNBA anyway. ✦

Chapter Twelve

I Am Woman Hear Me Jangle

"*Women here are very vivid in a way that surprised me. They express themselves colorfully.*"

—*Mary, Ohio, twelve years in Texas*

I sometimes worry that I don't know what it is to have a true friend because I have never been so glad to see anyone that I emitted the sort of ear-shattering shrill Texas sorority chicks let out when they run into each other.

"EEEEEEEEEEEEEE! HOW ARRRRRRREEE YEWW-WWWWWWW? EEEEEEEE!"

You would think they had been separated since birth although they might have last squealed and hugged just hours ago. Following the squealing comes a duet of exclamations about how CUTE! and DARLING! each other looks, escalating into an jab and parry of compliments and self-deprecation. "Oh, you always look so nice," "Oh, I've put on so much weight," "Oh, you're such a skinny thing, you never have to worry." "Oh but look how cute your hair looks," "Oh no, I didn't have time to do it today"...and so on and so on until all they can do is squeal and hug again. "It's so good to see yewwwwwww!" they agree.

This sort of alarming exuberance falls into the category of what writer Florence King identified as the "Pert Plague, that hyperkinetic frenzy that still exists in the South." Pertness is a southern specialty virtually unknown to Yankee chicks. Pertness is shrill-voiced, smiley-faced, scatter-brained, and fidgety. Pertness makes ponytails bob, skirts flounce, eyelashes flutter. Pertness declares everything "precious."

I couldn't pull off pert if you held a gun to my head. Texas chicks have honed pertness for generations. It's bigger than you or me or all the Yankee chicks that came before and will come after. Because the real secret of pertness is that it's a lie. Pert women come across as lightweights you could blow off with a puff of breath, but they know what they're doing.

Pertness was developed in the face of sexism. It is a costume women wear here to allow men to think them empty-headed while they secretly run the world behind the scenes. "I don't really understand the women here, but I think they have iron spines," says Cerie from L.A.

In *Dr. T. and the Women* the pert/powerful dichotomy is personified in Laura Dern's loveable Peggy, who drinks and dithers and runs around in silly clothes and hats. She also raises her children with care and love, and even though she has to pop into the bathroom for a nip now and then, she is clearly the rock of a family that is in crisis.

The frontier women of Texas were as hardy as frontier women anywhere, but they also bore a singular place in their society because they were the antithesis of life on the range. Cowboys didn't want to be fenced in, and women built fences. Cowboys did want to get laid, however, so they learned to cherish their women when they were home, and women learned to take care of themselves when they weren't. The Texas dream date is a woman like Lorena in *Lonesome Dove*, a sensual whore with a sexy little scar on her lip who isn't afraid of the great frontier. When Jake smacked Lorena's face for doing her business with Gus, "... there was not real anger in it ...," and it left just "a little red spot ... made no impression at all." It didn't make Lorena feel any worse about earning $50 from Gus, and Jake got over the affront pretty quickly and let her talk him into joining Call's cattle drive. She took the hit and yet won the point. Women are as strong as they are weak.

In one deliciously Texan moment in *The Alamo*, John Wayne/Davy Crockett lifts Flaca bodily and places her into the rickety cart in which she will escape the impending siege. He apparently considered Flaca capable of traversing a war zone in a donkey cart, but unable to board the wagon without his help.

Texas is a curious combination of gynocratic and sexist. Women are both put down and put up on pedestals; they are assumed to be tempered steel under their Mary Kay. "Until 1918, the state maintained a legal class consisting of 'idiots, aliens, the insane, and women' and it's been slow going ever since," wrote Molly Ivins. "...the good news is," she continues, "that all this adversity has certainly made us a bodacious bunch of overcomers. And rather pleasant as a group, I always think, since having a sense of humor about men is not a luxury here; it's a necessity." To play the game, women pretend to be weak and men pretend to believe them. But women can do without men a lot better, it seems, than men can do without women, and everyone knows it.

Lots of Texas chicks are Hell's Angels at heart. My boss at one job wore her hair loose and feminine, always kept it curled, and was never seen without enough mascara to be blinded in a rainstorm. I knew she was a hardy South Texas chick, but when she took me to see Clyde Barrow's grave in southern Dallas and we found the cemetery fenced off, I was unprepared to see Karen toss her handbag over the fence then hop over after it, as if she'd been trespassing all her life. I can hold my own in a New York subway in the wee hours, but I've never jumped a fence in my life. She had to help me over. And Karen and her husband once drove motorcycles from Texas to Canada. "It was fun," she said cheerfully. "Except for the bugs in my teeth."

At a barbecue recently, I witnessed a well-groomed, tanning booth bronze, taut-tummied young blonde—a genuine Dallas Cowboys Cheerleader candidate—daintily filling and refilling and refilling her plastic cup with a clear liquid poured from a flask she kept in her purse. She grew prettily and discreetly drunk, sipping her cocktails through a straw which is, a feminine East Texas chick once informed me, the secret to keeping your lipstick fresh through a long evening drinking. (You also will never see a proper Texas chick wrap her lips untidily around a longneck. She manages to sip even those daintily.) By late night this pretty cheerleader was clearly drunk but no less glistening, with lipstick intact and hair still holding a hot roller curl. I would put my money on her in a drinking contest with Dean Martin.

But though the Texas chick may drink like a cowboy, she must eat like a bird. In *Fixin' to Party, Texas Style* Helen Bryant cautions that at charity events, it is borderline acceptable for a husband to polish off his wife's unfinished desert if "it is a desert so fabulous you may never see its equal." However, she cautions, "Women, if you do this, you'll look like a pig! And you absolutely may not take your dessert—or any other part of your meal—home with you. You'll look like a pig!"

Texas chicks never want to look like pigs (nor, I concede, do Yankee chicks) and yet *killing* a pig can be considered a womanly endeavor in Texas. One friend boasts at length of his beautiful wife's hunting prowess. Their freezer already overflows with venison she has bagged. "Now she wants a wild pig," he says. "We know where there's a big one, 400 pounds. She wants it bad."

Tipping the seesaw again, we must note that though a woman can bag a 400-pound pig, she may be considered incapable of lifting a 50-pound bag. "My husband and I were buying 50-pound bags of sand," says Melanie. "I picked one up to put it in the car, and this sales guy pulls it away from me, staggering a little, saying 'No, no, you're just a fragile little thing. You can't carry that.'"

Proper Texas chicks follow a complex code of behavior. Tough business chicks in Texas dance an even trickier two-step. Mary Kay Ash, a prototype for a successful Texas woman, gamboled between ardent feminism and little ladyhood. In her 1995 book *You Can Have It All*, she urged women to succeed big while exhorting them to watch their dainty step.

"I've seen females become so aggressive in their climb up the corporate ladder, in their fervor to make law partner, or in their desire to be patted on the back by their sales manager, that they stop being ladies," she wrote. "In order to be accepted as 'one of the guys,' not only do they tolerate men using foul language in their presence, they lower their own standards. Soon...they may even lose the expression of their femininity by the way they dress. In their effort to imitate men, they compromise a major asset, their womanliness, and they are no longer good role models for their own daughters."

(Presumably Mary Kay never spent much time with congresswoman Barbara Jordan, who, in her autobiography, explained her attitude towards men and cussin'. "I didn't try to use salty language because that would make me one of them, but I just wanted them to be comfortable and not keep saying: 'Excuse me, pardon me,'" she said.)

Ebby Halliday, another well-coiffed and ladylike mogul, only in the past decade relaxed her company dress code to allow pantsuits on women, and only because she felt skirts were getting too short. Yet she is the acknowledged and adored queen of residential real estate in Dallas. And about Sarah Weddington, of Roe v. Wade fame, Ann Richards wrote, "what impressed me about Sarah Weddington is that she was pretty and feminine, and yet she talked about really tough issues involving women—and she made sense." That's the admiration of one Texas chick to another and the standards are high: pretty, feminine, *and* tough. You try it!

A Few Tough Texas Chicks to Admire

Barbara Jordan: Barbara Jordan and her sister both were raised in a restrictive church atmosphere ("I do not recall joy related to my experience of these years at church," Jordan said in *Barbara Jordan: A Self-Portrait*), but while her sister grew up to remain contained by home and church in traditional Texas fashion, Jordan rebelled all the way to the Senate, becoming the first black woman to address the National Democratic Convention. ("...two women in 160 years is about par for the course," Ann Richards pointed out twelve years later, when she was the convention's keynote speaker.) Jordan riveted the nation when she spoke her carefully considered mind at the Watergate hearings. "I believe hyperbole would not be fictional and would not overstate the solemnity that I feel right now," she said. "My faith in the Constitution is whole, it is complete, it is total. I am not going to sit here and be an idle spectator to the diminution, the subversion, the destruction of the Constitution." When she died in 1996, she became the first African-American buried in the Texas State Cemetery. Though Jordan had a female companion most of her life, she never came out publicly as a lesbian, and that side of her life remains delicately shrouded. Perhaps her many facets of difference from the southern lady—black, political, lesbian—freed her to buck society and break traditions.

Ann Richards: Ann Richards came and went quickly, in a couple of odd moments: her showstopper keynote speech at the Democratic convention and her victory in an ugly gubernatorial race against cartoon character Clayton Williams. She then lost the office to George W., with his good ol' boy backslapping and nicknames and presidential daddy.

But Ann Richards made progress. She gave a voice and a perfectly acceptable look to Texas feminism, and we love her for it. In an article titled "Ann Richards, Feminist, Role Model Prophet," in a UT publication titled *23,007* (for the number of women students at UT), one junior wrote about meeting Richards at an event. "I wanted to shake her hand firmly, look her in the eye, and connect with her, to let her know that the simple fact that she existed made me feel optimistic about politics, about women, about the world."

That's how Ann Richards makes me feel, too.

Here's just one reason to love Ann Richards, as told by Molly Ivins from *Molly Ivins Can't Say That, Can She?* and originally published in *Ms. Magazine* in 1988:

Molly Ivins, state comptroller Bob Bullock, Ann Richards, and a black man named Charles Miles, who headed Bullock's personnel department, were sitting together at a political hoop-de-do when they were approached by what Ivins calls, "a dreadful old racist judge from East Texas."

I'll let Molly take it from there:

"Judge," said Bullock. "I want you to meet my friends. This is Molly Ivins with the *Texas Observer*."

The judge peered at me and said, "How yew, little lady?"

"This is Charles Miles, who heads my personnel department."

Charles stuck out his hand and the judge got an expression on his face as though he had just stepped into a fresh cowpie. It took him a long minute before he reached out, barely touched Charlie's hand, and said, "How yew, *boy*?" Then he turned with great relief to pretty, blue-eyed Ann Richards and said, "And who is this lovely lady?"

Ann beamed and said, "I am Mrs. Miles."

Molly Ivins: (who, it must be admitted, was born in California but grew up in Houston) ignores what's considered proper for a lady and opens her liberal feminist trap on any topic she chooses, and Texans love her anyway. (At least the few remaining liberals do. I suppose conservatives might prefer the views of Senator Kay Bailey Hutchison, another tough Texas chick with immobile hair.) I won't even try to address Texas politics in this book because I could study the topic for a lifetime and still never say anything Molly Ivins hasn't said before and better. She called Ross Perot "all hawk and no spit." How could I ever top that? Molly Ivins can say things that would get a carpetbagger like me rode back to damn Yankee-land on the tines of a pitchfork.

Hallie Stillwell: I had the privilege of meeting Hallie Stillwell once, as even in advanced age, Hallie often held court in her family's trailer park. Hallie settled in West Texas in 1916, survived what may have been the nation's harshest frontier, killed a cougar with one shot between the eyes, was the first woman to work on the city desk of a newspaper in Texas, and generally earned her legend in dozens of ways. Her passing, in 1997 just months short of her 100th birthday, was mourned statewide. Hallie's Hall of Fame Museum is worth a visit, and she wrote an entertaining autobiography, titled *I'll Gather My Geese*. Hallie is not nationally famous, but she was the quintessential Texas tough cookie.

Mary Kay: Her Pinkness is the chick entrepreneur extraordinaire, making her considerable fortune with cosmetics, pink Cadillacs, and the company motto: "God first, family second, career third." Mary Kay Ash started her company with her life savings of $5,000 in 1953. In 2000 the company made more than $2.5 billion in retail sales. Mary Kay built her business when women didn't do things like that, when she was still required to hurry home and be waiting when her husband got home. Mary Kay has a charitable foundation focusing on cancer research and violence against women. We should all be such delicate pink blossoms. ◆

In some ways, Yankee chicks who do not feel bound by niceness can use their Yankeeness to an advantage in business, provided they are not so blunt as to shut people down. Pam says she learned to tone down her opinions at work after discovering that her colleagues were speculating on ways to oust her. But Anne, a newspaper reporter, finds her Yankee spunk helps her push past the condescension of Texas Bubbas by allowing her to lob hardball questions and not get now-now-little-lady-ed out of answers. "Either they get pissed off, or they start answering my questions, but either way they take me more seriously," Anne says. "I wonder how girls from Texas do that. I don't see them pushing like that. I guess they must have another way."

Texas women do have their own interesting methods for getting their way. You could call it manipulation or you could call it people skills, but women here are rarely as fluffy as they look. Gloria Steinem, asked about people she would like to interview, replied, "Mostly, I'd like to do ordinary women, like those of Longview, Texas. They wear jeans and boots on the bottom, with these frilly blouses and faces full of makeup on top. And they are tough!"

When Adlai Stevenson, U.S. ambassador to the United Nations, spoke in Dallas in 1962, an organized contingent of anti-U.N. women jangled their charm bracelets every time he opened his mouth, ultimately forcing him off the stage. Among other delightful elements of this anecdote is the fact that there were enough charm bracelets in Dallas to drown out a politician.

Texas chicks hold their own sort of power in their strong and well-manicured hands. Mary, who runs in circles where few women work, says, "Women run the households here. When the men walk in it's her domain and the man has got to step to it. His job is to bring the money in, but the house is hers."

"And women really do run the church here," say Judy. "Where I grew up, that wasn't the case."

"And I have never met so many women with advanced degrees who could be running companies but don't work and are chomping at the bit," Kim adds.

These educated homemakers instead flex their executive muscle in charity work. It is a grave mistake to underestimate the Junior League, which is run like a major corporation by tough-minded blossoms. Mary, a member of the league, describes it as noblesse oblige and recalls being called upon to tackle a time-consuming job. "The committee chair didn't ask if I had time, she just told me what I had to do." Charity organizations feverishly woo the Junior League because the well-groomed group is capable of rallying armies of volunteers and pots of money for causes they deem worthy. Raising and dishing out the kinds of dollar amounts major Texas charities provide is no small-potatoes operation. When I worked for a nonprofit, few things struck fear in the board more than making a presentation to the Crystal Charities, one of Dallas' major charitable organizations run by the doyennes of Dallas' power families. The women who make the money decisions are taut and tan, impeccably dressed, bejeweled, exquisitely polite, steely, and smart. They might have names like stuffed animals: Fluffy, Bunny, or Twinkle (all real names of real society chicks), but they are not to be underestimated.

Even garden clubs are more than ladies in white gloves and floppy hats. The ladies of the Jesse Wise Garden Club in Jefferson, Texas, saved that town from decay with the bed and breakfast-ication of the town's collection of Victorian mansions. The Tyler Garden Club Texas gave birth to that city's premier annual event, the Rose Festival, which brings thousands of tourists to Tyler each year. The centerpiece of the festival is the Rose Parade, in which the Rose Queen and her court—local debutantes—ride through town on floats, surrounded by marching bands and cheerleaders.

Texas chicks must be businesswomen and beauty queens and still let men think it's a man's world. On a Dallas radio show, the morning drive-time deejay teased one of his cohorts about her "bubble butt." The hair on the back of my neck stood up immediately, but the woman merely retorted that she hoped that wouldn't be what people noticed about her first. "What would you want them to notice?" the deejay asked. She thought a minute and responded, "That I'm nice."

Being nice at all times is key to Texas womanhood, even in the face of sexism that makes Yankee chicks want to run with the Amazons. In *Honeysuckle Rose,* a Willie Nelson road movie, Amy Irving interprets a Texas chick by grinning like a ninny through most of the movie, even when the guys in the band joke about putting her college education to the test by making her fetch beers. For a moment I thought she'd protest, but she just grinned some more and got the beer, and Willie Nelson loved her for it, even though he had Dyan Canon, poured into her western wear, waiting faithfully for him at home. (Amy Irving made a very weird Texas chick. She was far more convincing as a New York City Jewish girl in *Crossing Delancey.* Jewish Yankee chick Debra Winger, however, was a great Texan in *Urban Cowboy.* She apparently got the part after real Texas chick—and real Sissy—Sissy Spacek didn't hit it off with John Travolta in their first meeting.)

To live in Texas you must simply become inured to a certain amount of institutionalized sexism, though you can sometimes indulge your Yankee right to bitch. I was impelled to write a letter to *The Dallas Morning News* when a long front-page article examined the racial make-up of the membership of the city's four top country clubs, mentioning only in passing that three of the four clubs do not allow women as full members. Women, it seems, must be wed to members, although this fact was apparently unremarkable enough to warrant no further comment in the article. The response I received from the paper acknowledged "unspoken" discrimination towards women. Unspoken? If it's in the club bylaws, it's very much spoken. I have not gotten to the bottom of this maddeningly retro policy but suspect the country club wives fear successful, unmarried women running around in tennis skirts might distract their husbands. (Witness the havoc free spirit Helen Hunt wreaks in *Dr. T.*)

Blatantly modern women are sometimes eyed with suspicion here. When a Texan friend prepared to wed, I asked if she would be changing her lovely Cajun name. "Yeeeees," she said coyly, knowing I'd opted not to take my husband's name. "I love *my* husband." I'm sure she didn't mean it as it sounded, bless my heart.

Holly, who also did not change her name, applied for a joint bank account for herself and her husband when she first arrived in Texas. "I moved straight from feminist radical lesbian Barnard College to Abilene, Texas," she says. "I wanted both our names on the account. I sat at the little desk—Bill wasn't there—and the lady with very sculpted hair and beady little eyes says, 'Uh-huh, mmm, uhhh, now, what is the relationship between you and Bill?'"

Holly responded with good old Yankee testiness. "I said, 'You know what? It's none of your goddam business what it is,' It took my breath away that someone would even ask me that."

Twenty years later this situation is surely less likely to occur, and if it did, Holly would respond with more diplomacy. "I was naive in my New Yorkness, I guess," she says. "After that I knew I had to tread a little more carefully."

You don't exactly get used to this kind of stuff, you just stop fighting it in the small arenas. You get used to being called "honey" and other kindly meant but belittling blandishments, although they are grating in some circumstances. "I definitely don't go for 'honey' and 'sweetie' in the business world," says Rett, from New Jersey, who has been in Texas twelve years. And you learn to cope with the sheen of little ladyhood that is applied to Texas life. You know it's not the whole story. And in some ways, you have to admit, it's not always that bad. "When I'm on a date, even in my car, the guy always pumps the gas," says Pat. "I feel a little guilty, but I've gotten used to it."

Chapter Thirteen

Underdressed, Overdressed, and In-Between

*"Floral print dresses with white collars.
I never saw that before."*

—Karen, L.A., ten years in Texas

*O*n my first visit to Texas, I saw a woman outside a convenience store shockingly dressed in shorts, spaghetti-strap tank top, and sandals. She looked so naked, I wanted to throw a jacket around her and hurry her home to change. If you exposed that much skin on the streets of New York, you would cause a riot. Then I lived through my first Texas summer and understood that the skimpy outfit was neither shocking nor inappropriate. Now I spend several months of the year in shorts and tank tops. It's hot here.

Texans have a whole different relationship with shorts than Yankees do. I was talking to a friend in New Jersey recently when he made reference to wearing what he called "short pants." This sounded quaint to me, but I recall that in my New York years, I rarely wore shorts except for some specific, vaguely athletic event (i.e., going to Central Park to lackadaisically toss a Frisbee). But here, shorts are a wardrobe staple. As Inuits have hundreds of words for snow, so do Texans have a full vocabulary of shorts: jogging shorts; soccer shorts; cut-offs, khakis; coach shorts (polyester, ugly); skorts (half shorts, half skirt); short-shorts. These terms are, of course, not exclusive to Texas but are perhaps more widely used here since you can wear shorts in nearly any situation and most times of the year. "One of my favorite things is that if the weather is over 40 degrees, you can wear shorts," says Andrea from Oregon. You can dress shorts down or up. You can get away with wearing shorts and heels if you do it right (low heels, preferably sandals). I like the sassy style of cutoffs and cowboy boots.

Sundresses (a.k.a. "little sundresses") are another wardrobe staple, and you can get away with them about anywhere. You see them in offices, perhaps formalized with a little jacket or cardigan; at the supermarket; at the symphony. They are cotton, linen, or rayon, short or long, floral print (a southern favorite) or solid color, and feminine. You'll even see punk rockers traipsing around in flimsy little nothings worn with clunky Doc Martens.

It's all about the temperature.

Looking fabulous in the summer heat (or at least not like a drowned raccoon) must be learned and mastered. "Is it just me, or does no other woman sweat on her face?" Pat asks desperately. Living in torpid Houston, Pat has a particular challenge. "During the summer if I put my make-up on for work, by the time I get in, the base and blush have dripped down my neck onto my shirt, my mascara makes me look like a raccoon, my powdered eye shadow has disappeared save for what's all wadding up in the creases above my eyes, and my lipstick is on my chin, fingers, hair, and forehead. Am I just not genetically predisposed to living in this climate? I now keep a bag of make-up at work. Once I get into air conditioning, I put it on. Of course my car has a/c, but it's that short walk to and from the car."

We all learn our tricks for surviving the heat looking, if not great, then not awful. Yankee chicks may not, in fact, be genetically disposed to this climate. We sweat, whereas Texas women only glow.

Work with it. Go easy on the make-up. Stick to concealer, powder, mascara, and maybe eye pencil, blush, and lipstick if you're going all out. If you must use foundation, use oil-free. Karen from L.A. once was known for her elaborate eye shadow, but now she limits her cosmetics to lipstick. "I never even filled in the gaps on all the make-up that's melted," she says.

Dressing right starts at your most intimate parts: cotton panties. The next layer should be breezy. Cotton, linen, lightweight, loose fitting, sleeveless, breathable, and comfortable. The first accessory I discarded were all my wide cinch belts. Nothing is less comfortable than a stiffly non-breathable accessory binding your middle.

Pantyhose are a necessity in some offices, optional in others. Karen, who lives in San Antonio, says her town is far less stylish and clothing-conscious than Dallas or Houston. "The plus side of that is I have not worn pantyhose one single time since I moved here. Yahoo!" While pantyhose in winter are no problem, they are cruel and unusual in Texas summer heat. When I worked in a pantyhose office, the first thing I did upon stepping in the door at the end of the day was tear the terrible things off. One woman I know doesn't even make it that far; her pantyhose come off as soon as she gets in her car. If you work in a pantyhose office (for example, the Dallas public schools require teachers to wear them), all sympathy. I can't help you. Find a new job.

Bare arms are acceptable in many workplaces here, although you may regret them when you arrive at the office and immediately turn purple in the a/c. This accounts for outbreaks of ugly sweaters in offices all over Texas, as most women keep an unsavory, misshapen, pilled sweater in the bottom file drawer of their desks to pull on when the a/c gets tough.

In summer I go for cotton and rayon pants, dresses, and skirts with little cotton tops. (Much of what you wear here is referred to in the diminutive: little dresses, little tops, little denim skirts.) Jeans are virtually impossible from late spring until autumn, unless you're going to a C&W club, in which case you'll have to cram yourself into the tightest ones you can find and suffer the sweatiness. (Note, by the way, that real kicker chicks wear round-toed ropers not Ralph Lauren-esque pointy-toed boots. You also can choose to be frilly on the dance floor, with a prairie skirt look.)

The last accessory you must consider in the heat is your car. You can be dressed to beautiful breezy perfection, but if your car is an Easy-Bake Oven, you'll be a sticky mess before you're out of the driveway. During one carless stint, a friend loaned me his un-air-conditioned car to run some errands. When I heard a couple of teenage girls behind me in line at the 7-11 giggling, I realized I was so sweaty, my flowered underwear was showing through my cotton drawstring pants.

Buy a light-colored car. Use a folding sunshield across the windshield and crack your windows when you park. Park in the shade whenever possible.

You may also need to rethink your shopping habits. Fashion here is dictated more by the calendar than the thermometer, which means you might think it's summer but if Madison Avenue says it's fall, that's what the stores carry. Laura says she looked around a business meeting one fall day and realized all the women were wearing Shetland sweaters. "It was, like, a million degrees out," she says. Yankee chicks invariably make the mistake of looking for summer clothes as soon as the weather starts warming up, around March, and are dismayed to find the stores still full of long-sleeved tops and jeans. The best time to shop for the coming summer is the autumn before, when last summer's clothes are all on sale. Fall clothes start appearing in the stores in August, when an end to summer's heat is still months away.

And, yes, fashions here are behind the Coasts. I stock up on trends when visiting New York, L.A., or London. "I joke that I was able to wear all the clothes I brought from New York for four years, because it takes that long for fashions to come down here," says Pat. That's not completely a joke. A quick out-of-town shopping trip can put you ahead of the fashion curve down here, if that's important to you.

Every event has its own informal dress code, of course. I treated my first barbecue as I would have a New York party and got all dolled up in nightclub drag: black clothes, eye make-up, lipstick. I looked like the town trollop; everyone else was in shorts and tank tops. (It's the temperature, stupid.) Underdressing for a barbecue is nearly impossible.

In Dallas and Houston, it's difficult to be overdressed for any event that takes place indoors. I've gone to stinky sports bars full of guys in Dockers, and half the women are in heels and hairspray. In Lubbock, it's probably pretty easy to overdo it. As Helen Bryant explains in *Fixin' to Party, Texas Style*, Dallas and Houston daytime clothes can pass as evening wear in Lubbock or Austin, which are more denim-centric.

But what of the dreaded "Dressy Casual" edict on an invitation? "Stockings, absolutely!" Bryant writes. "And expensive slacks with a silk shirt and pearls. No, there's nothing casual about it. But it's a way of telling you to limit the jewel encrustation." Those of us whose jewel encrustation is naturally limited appreciate the permission.

Some events are anarchy; at the symphony and theater, you'll see everything from sequins to jeans. (That's not much different from anyplace else. I heard a Dallas DJ tell about going to her first Broadway show with her sister. They got all done up in sequins and sheer black hose and little strappy sandals. "We looked like idiots," she said.) If you feel like wearing an evening gown to see the touring company of *Les Miz*, you might not be alone in the crowd, but the riffraff in the balcony will probably be in little sundresses.

Oh, and one nifty shopping secret I've learned is to figure out the charities the high rollers favor and see if they have thrift stores attached to them. At these, you'll often find last year's once-worn fabulous outfits, donated by compassionate, well-dressed rich ladies who can't be seen in the same outfit twice. Consignment stores are perfectly acceptable, too. Like in Los Angeles, people do it, even if they don't talk about it.

A word about winter. "Texans are in total denial about the temperature," says Lucy, who walked into Starbucks once in Boston-style coat, gloves, hat, and scarf and was horrified to see everyone else in lightweight coats.

"I have a coat problem," says Holly. "I've gotten rid of all my coats." Full-length coats are unnecessary down here. So is heavy wool anything. Winter wear is long-sleeved tops, light wool or heavy cotton knits, sweaters, car coats, sometimes hat, scarf, and gloves but nothing serious. Just layer until it feels right, you probably won't be outside any longer than it takes to get from car to building anyway. Dressing for winter is a non-issue. Undressing for summer is a lot more difficult.

Chapter Fourteen

Yes Ma'am, I Would Like To Tear Your Clothes Off, If You Don't Mind

"You do have to be open to being called 'darlin'.' "It isn't derogatory in their frame of reference. After the first few times, the hair on my arms stopped standing up every time he said it."

—*Laura, Iowa, three years in Texas*

I once found myself in a relationship with a Texan entirely by accident. It all started after a date, when he was so polite about asking to "sleep over," I thought he actually intended to sleep. By the time I realized my mistake, I was too embarrassed to admit it. It actually took me a couple of months to extricate myself from what developed from that point.

I dated another Texan for several months without understanding that we were, in fact, dating. Poor fellow, I cringe to think of it. He drove at least 30 minutes each way to see me and never got so much as a peck on the cheek. He was so polite, I thought we were just friends. It wasn't until he stopped coming around and finally called to announce—with a tinge of vindication in his voice—that he was getting married, that his take on the "friendship" occurred to me.

Apparently, I'm not qualified to give advice on dating Texas men. I married a Yankee who's as plainspoken and ornery as I am. But I like Texas men and so do other Yankee chicks. "They're respectful and definite guy-guys, in a good way," says Dana from New York.

"I think cowboys are completely sexy," says Karen. "They respect land, animals, and women. And not just to get a date, but because it's the right thing to do."

Yankee chicks sometimes come to Texas with dreams of cowboys dancing in their heads, then find Texas men come in all flavors, Bubbas to poets. (I dated a Texan poet for a while, about which Yankee husband says, "A POET!? *Haw, haw haw!* A POET?") Some Texas guys I've known: John, who cooks and cleans and loves Broadway musicals but is straight and loves women so much, he was (before he married) genuinely hurt that he couldn't keep all his ex-lovers as friends. Russell, who appreciated equally Toni Morrison, Patti Smith, Costa Rica, old movies, George Jones, and football. Tommy, who lived for a time in a trailer on a flea market across the street from a drag strip and works in human services for the state. Frank, a minister's son who was a Peace Corps volunteer in Honduras before settling in the neighborhood where he grew up, near his parents. Greg, an artist and animal rights activist. George, a history teacher with a trust fund who lives in the house in which he grew up. Kim, who thinks of himself as "the David Niven of Bonham, Texas" and is capable of shocking bawdiness but also is first to notice and compliment a girl if she's wearing something new. Philip, a construction worker and guitar picker who just isn't himself if he doesn't get his daily dose of Tai Chi.

Texas men are as varied as Yankee chicks are. But whatever their other proclivities, Texas men, reared by mamas they worship in a culture that places women on a pedestal, are often exquisitely gallant. "Liz Taylor, next to my wife, was the most beautiful woman in the world," said Texan Bob Hinkle in *Return to Giant*, a documentary about the making of the classic Texas movie. Hinkle was dialogue coach for James Dean and Rock Hudson, but he also could clearly teach any Yankee a thing or two about making women glow. I'd guess his wife is not actually more beautiful than Liz Taylor, but I'll bet she feels like she is. I have never met a New Yorker who would even try to pull off such enchanting flattery. The guys I know in New York are more likely to pride themselves on their egalitarian attitude towards women. But the Yankee chick's guilty little secret is that it is actually nice to be treated like a little lady sometimes. Texas men pump your gas, hold doors, and call you "young lady" even if you're neither. "I worked in a high rise and

I kept missing my floor, because I waited for everyone to get off and they were all waiting for me to get off," says Pat.

"After six months in Texas I went to D.C. and almost had a door slam in my face because I was so used to men holding open the door and me waltzing through," says Anne. The gentlemanly stuff can feel awkward at first, but you will get used to it. I don't even mind being called "darlin'" sometimes.

Guy Haunts

One of the best places to find large quantities of a surprising variety of Texas men is at sporting events. Yes, you'll encounter drunken fools with their faces painted in team colors, but I also know artists, musicians, and public broadcasting executives who never turn down tickets to a Dallas Stars hockey game. In San Antonio, where there's not much to do, Spurs games are something to do. Houston suffered the deep humiliation of losing its football team to Nashville but has rallied with a new NFL team, the Houston Texans, debuting in 2002. And the Houston Comets are national basketball champs, though the WNBA still attracts more women fans than men. Sports bars and bars with big TVs also attract quantities of shiny young men and women on game nights, especially when Texas teams are in championship playoffs. The mingling here is particularly easy if you actually know something about the sport.

If you're determined to find a cowboy, learn how to two-step (lots of clubs give free lessons early in the evening) and hang out at country music clubs. Dancing cowboys love dancing and aren't shy about asking. If you can two-step you'll have your choice of sweet-smelling guys in hats and jeans. And line dancing can get you on the floor and looking cute even if you have no partner. The most urban cowboy clubs play disco, too, and it's a hoot 'n' a holler watching cowboys dance to "Funky Cold Medina." Guys who follow Texas roots music—cowboys of a somewhat different ilk—flock to historic dance halls throughout the state, where those acts often play.

Otherwise, meeting men in Texas is like anywhere else. Joyce met her Texan husband on a fix-up. Melanie met hers by running a personal ad. Cerie, a former flight attendant, met hers on a flight. Laura did it Texas-style, joining a club of sorts: It was a dating service and after a lot of near misses, she may have hit a winner. (And it only takes one, right?) I met my Yankee husband at a barbecue. Texas is full of eligible men. Get out there and bat some lash. ✦

Texas men also tend to be the marrying kind. Raised in close families, they often are anxious to re-create their own childhood homes. Men want to marry, buy a nest, let their women feather it, and start cranking out little Billy Bud Juniors. And in Texas, despite the machismo, there is no shame when a man calls his wife "the boss." In matters domestic, Texas husbands respect and usually defer to the power of wives. (The drawback to this for men, though, is that they in turn are expected to be willing and proficient in all the manly arts.

Texan John is incensed anytime someone assumes that because he is a man, he has any idea at all what's going on under the hood of his car.) All in all, Texas men are a good deal. They're gentlemanly, they're masculine, they cook, they take out the garbage, they cut the grass, they're nice to your mother.

Texans You Could Bring Home to Mama

Nolan Ryan, record-breaking pitcher: Confident, courtly, quiet, and serious about his job—an athlete with dignity and humility. Plus, man enough to beat up a guy half his age who charged him on the mound.

Colby Donaldson, media darling: The *Survivor* golden boy double dealt with the best of them, cried with love for his mama, and gallantly tossed the game to Tina. Quintessential Texas good boy/bad boy.

Lance Armstrong, cyclist and real survivor: Plano boy makes good despite overwhelming odds. Strong, talented, sensitive family man. Cuddles his infant son publicly.

George Strait, white-hatted country crooner: The cowboy you wish would lean over and say, "Excuse me, darlin', would you care to dance?"

Lyle Lovett, tall-haired singer/songwriter: So peculiar, it's hard to believe he's Texan. ♦

The only thing Texas men seem to lack since they've been dragged from the frontier to the city is a sense of style. They're clean and well groomed, even fussy. At the dry cleaner once, I watched a young man explain to the proprietor how to press his massive baggy jeans. He put them on and the cuffs hung in puddles on the floor, but the young man carefully indicated exactly where the crease should fall. But however crisp, the look for thirty-something-and-up guys who want to fit in is, frankly, uninspired: khaki shorts or slacks and plaid or striped sports shirts. There's nothing wrong with this look, but if what you wear makes a statement about who you are, then this outfit says, "Indistinguishable from the next guy." I once spent an evening at a groovy downtown Dallas bar where all the women were dazzling in little black dresses with leopard accessories, gold jewelry, stiletto-heeled sandals, and hair for days. Meanwhile the guys, to the man, wore khaki shorts or slacks, sport shirts, and baseball caps. This is dispiriting, and you must remind yourself that there really is a different fellow in each pair of Dockers.

Perhaps men don't dress up because women do. At her physical therapist's office, Kim from New York followed a conversation between two boots-and-jeans Texans about what to wear to an upcoming afternoon wedding. They finally concluded it didn't matter what they wore. "After about four weeks, they decided that as long as their women looked good, that was good enough," Kim recalls. It's a lot easier to accessorize with a great-looking woman than put on a tux.

It's not that men here aren't vain, they just can't appear to work at it. Dallas Cowboys owner Jerry Jones made front-page news when he lost weight and got a facelift. Or at least he appears to have had a facelift. He won't say for sure because a facelift wouldn't be manly. It's a strange anomaly that so many Texas men prove they're not wussies by dressing like weenies, filling their wardrobes with identical pants and shirts rather than experimenting with fashion.

Perhaps a lot of guys also don't knock themselves out because guys don't need to be dazzling for women to act dazzled. If a guy is a guy, it doesn't matter what he's wearing, someone will flirt with him. "Southern women flirt so automatically that half the time they don't even realize they are doing it," Florence King explains. "Batting your lashes is a Pavlovian reaction as soon as you say word one to any man, and so is that rapt gaze called 'hanging onto his every word.' In the South, it's all a game and everyone plays it; there are ways to make it clear that you are serious; you increase or decrease the watts and voltage depending upon how you *really* feel and what, if anything, you want the man to do about it. Southern men know the difference; northern men do not (understandably, since northern women, especially New Yorkers, don't carry on in this fashion)."

While I don't suggest Yankee chicks are incapable of flirting, I propose only a gifted few have honed the art as southern women have. "No contest," says Linda from Pennsylvania about her skills as compared to Texans. "What they seem to be able to do that I never mastered is keep clear that it's just a game. A Texan guy seems to know the rules as well as a Texan gal; they play along and don't go getting all serious about it. It seems just as choreographed a dance as the Cotton-Eyed Joe."

I don't think my eyelashes are physiologically capable of batting, though I have seen it done to great effect by southern women. And a Texas woman's smile has more wattage than the Las Vegas strip. When she directs it at men, they are blinded to all else. You can't blame them. Generations of training went into that smile.

A Word About Texans and Guns

More than one Yankee chick has been stunned to learn that the Texan who is wooing her keeps firearms. Gun ownership is not limited to Bubbas or even guys. Women also proudly pack heat. But guns may be the Grand Canyon of cultural divides between Yankee chicks and Texans. Yankee chicks usually remember the first time they see the sign in a bar cautioning that carrying firearms is illegal where liquor is served. It's not that we're sorry the sign is there; it's just unnerving to realize you're among people who might have reason to be reminded of this law.

Melanie from New Jersey says guns are an unspoken, off-limits topic of discussion in her marriage to a Texan. When the concealed handgun law was passed in Texas, Maggie's father called her from St. Louis and demanded to know what was going on. I was horrified when one of my New Year's Eve parties ended with a friend shooting out the stop sign on my corner. (Fortunately this friend is considerably less volatile since he's been on the wagon. He does still love his guns, though.)

You just have to get used to it.

Texans put a lot of stake in the romance of the old frontier, and packing a pistol is part of that mystique.

While the frontier itself is being built over with Super-Targets, fenced off in gated communities, and parceled out to high-tech high rollers, Texans cling urgently to what they can of frontier life, including guns. (Also chewing tobacco, cowboy boots, and flesh roasted over an open fire.) Trying to debate guns with a Texan will only serve as a reminder that you're a damn Yankee coming down here trying to change everything. I suspect some Texans carry guns so when secession finally gets off the ground, they'll be ready.

Then there's the hunting thing.

While westerners and midwesterners may be at ease with a passion for hunting, the sport puts some Yankee chicks in a lather. "What is the deal with hunting?" said Pat, from Massachusetts. "You feed the deer all winter. Then you go to somebody's land and you sit in a shade thing—there's no exercise, there's no sport—and you wait until some friggin' thing comes over and you shoot it." (In fact, many states don't allow deer hunting over bait. Texas does.)

Hunting also is part of the frontier nostalgia. "If a woman ever stumbled onto this outfit at this hour of the day, she'd screech and poke out her eyes," said Gus as the men of *Lonesome Dove* stumbled groggily and grubbily to the breakfast table. You can trace a direct line from this moment to Richard Gere eating cheese sandwiches and crouching in a duck blind with his buddies in *Dr. T. and the Women*. This time spent hunting is about the only time Dr. T., a gynecologist and father of girls, is not surrounded by shrieking women. Although women do hunt, the popularity of hunting is as much about being manly as it is about shooting things. Texas men hunt to prove they're still men, even though the womenfolk at home make them sleep on feather pillows and eat with knives and forks. My husband went on a dove-hunting weekend once. What he remembers most vividly is a bean-heavy dinner and a long evening of guys farting loudly at will.

Hunting and guns are, if you'll excuse me, loaded issues for Yankees and Texans. Unless you're a deeply committed activist, leave it alone. Don't bother debating these issues. You'll just be shouted down by people packing heat.

Friendship between men and women may happen a little more easily back East because we are not weaned on flirtation and can more easily relax and forget that we have parts that fit together. Twice, not long after I moved down, I embarrassed myself by trying to maintain friendships with men after their relationships broke up. I was suspected of moving in like a heat-seeking predator, trying to snap up these newly "available" men. Incredibly, that interpretation of my actions didn't occur to me at the time. I was so accustomed to having romance-free friendships with guys back home, I honestly didn't think about how it might appear when I chose to call the male of the former couple, thinking I could be a good buddy and lend a sympathetic ear. I still blush to think of it now, many years later.

When it came to sexual intrigue back in New York, I was less likely to bat my eyelashes and beam than to rely on earnest and mysterious, hoping to attract dark and cynical New York guys. But earnest and mysterious don't play down here in Texas. Guys in clubs here were always urging me to "Smile!"

All in all, I was a mess when it came to the boy-girl game in Texas. It's a good thing Tom came along or I'd probably still be sulking in nightclub corners.

Pat did hook up with a true Texan but hit cultural bumps after they started dating. She was his first Yankee girlfriend. "I thought he was adorable but he broke up with me," Pat says. "I was too abrasive. He was acutely aware that I don't wear sundresses in summer. You have to have a manicure. You have to have make-up on at all times. I couldn't burp, I couldn't swear, I had to be in perfect shape even though he had a gut."

Of course, some Yankee-Texas unions are happily ever after. Joyce is blissfully married to a boots-and-jeans Texan she met after moving from Ohio, though she insisted he sell his guns before she would move in with him. And while they disagree on politics, they agree on everything else that matters, except two-stepping, which he loves and she doesn't. "When we go to clubs, he dances with other women. It's kind of odd, but I just don't like the C&W thing," Joyce says. And Joyce still butts heads with her conservative in-laws. "I'm not very good about keeping my mouth shut and my opinions to myself, especially when it comes to politics and Rush Limbaugh," she says.

Melanie from Maryland never had any problems with her in-laws, and she and her husband straddle not only the Mason-Dixon line, but also color lines. "His family has been wonderful," Melanie says. "There have been no clashes, white or black or culturally. His mother was exceptionally liberal. When I met her, she was elderly and infirm and spent her days watching CNN and railing against conservatives."

Laura is dating a pilot from Fort Worth, and although he didn't make her tingle at first, his calm and confident persistence won her over. He didn't even flinch when she canceled their second date at the last minute (her excuse was that the cable guy kept her waiting, which sounds fishy to me), and she was late for the third. He just persisted. "I guess when you wear the 'hero suit' (that's what he calls the pilot's uniform) you aren't used to getting no for an answer," Laura says. Soon Laura was known as "That Dallas Woman" to all her boyfriend's Fort Worth friends. He took her to see Jerry Jeff Walker, she took him to an Irish music show, all in the spirit of compromise and cross-cultural communications.

One of the most attractive things about Texas men is their confidence. Living in a society that sends them no mixed messages about feminine sides and junk like that, Texas men know exactly how they are supposed to behave and don't seem fearful of missteps. No Paul Reiser dithering for them. Texas men will try to sweep you off your feet, and if it doesn't work, they'll have a few beers and move on. If they're crying on the inside, it doesn't show. If they're nervous, you can't really tell.

Yes, Texas men can charm you into a limp noodle with their courtly manners and sweet-talking ways. But Yankee chicks, heed my warning. When they say "sleep over" they're not talking about sleep. Those smooth talkers are easy to bring home to mama, but don't imagine fine manners are a sure sign of pure motives. Don't forget that topless bars are big business in Texas. Clubs in Houston and Dallas are listed on NASDAQ, and dancers can make upwards of $100,000 a year. These bars are called "gentlemen's clubs," which leaves doubt in my mind as to how Texans define "gentlemen." And they also provide a hint of one of the more interesting anomalies of Texas men.

John Anders, a long-time columnist for *The Dallas Morning News* is a born and reared Texan and describes himself as "a sit-this-one-out, gum-chewing, canasta-playing, pineapple upside-down-cake-eating Baptist." Anders nailed the Baptist boy gestalt in a column that related to a comment from a woman he met in college. "Yeah, I know all about you Baptist boys," she said. "You're the ones who say 'yes sir' and 'no sir' to a girl's father like Eddie Haskell did. Then when you get us alone you try to chew the rivets off our jeans."

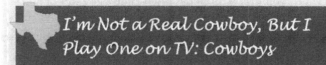

I'm Not a Real Cowboy, But I Play One on TV: Cowboys

Cowboys, the real thing, are nearly extinct. You will find men who have grown up in the big parts of Texas, who wear jeans and smell of horses and keep cows and call you little lady and swagger like cowboys, but chances are slim-to-zero they live a life on the range. The cattle drive ended in the last third of the nineteenth century, when barbed wire (a.k.a. "bob wahr") blocked the way and allowed cattle to graze wider swaths of land, and refrigerated train cars eliminated the need to move meat on the hoof. Today, a full-time cowboy is as likely to be hoisting tourists up onto somnambulistic steeds at a dude ranch as roping calves, unless he's a rodeo cowboy. The cowboy has become superfluous, no longer a cog in the nation's food industry. But he lives on all the same, like the longhorns in *Hud*. "I just keep 'em around for old times' sake," Granddad (Melvyn Douglas) says. "Keep 'em to remind me of how things was."

The King Ranch in South Texas, which at 825,000 acres is larger than the state of Rhode Island, remains a working ranch in a sense, and cattle still roam its acres, but it also has diversified into citrus groves, sugar cane fields, recreational hunting, tourism, printing, even a retail luggage business. Cowboys just ain't what they used to be.

"Lots of San Antonians have ranches with livestock, but they live in the city and have jobs—a landscaper, a city administrator, a mayor or two. I no longer think that just because you wear boots and a Stetson, you're a cowboy," says Anne, disillusioned after just two years in Texas.

Today's Texan is more likely to take a meeting than rope a calf, yet Texas (with the help of an adoring world) clings to the cowboy mystique. "...killing the myth of the cowboy is like trying to kill a snapping turtle; no matter what you do, the beast retains a sluggish life," McMurtry wrote.

Why is that?

Because cowboys are soooooooo sexy.

I am surely not the only single Yankee chick who moved to Texas thinking she might find herself one of them thar sexy cowboys. (And ended up with another Yankee instead.) Seen Paul Newman in *Hud?* OK, yes, it is Paul Newman, and he is a snake-in-the-grass who is hellbent on coming to a bad end, but when I closed my eyes and imagined the cowboy I'd like to run off with, he looked a lot like Hud. Patricia Neal has willpower of steel to resist the charms he pours on her, while he's dressed in hat and jeans and a tight snap-front shirt, no less. As Debra Winger says in *Urban Cowboy*, right before popping open the snaps of her bad-boy cowboy's shirt, "This is mah fav'rite thang." Sure, I enjoy the volubility of the New York intellectuals, but fiddling with those tiny buttons on an Oxford cloth shirt just isn't the same. And there's a reason that chaps are fetish-wear. And how sexy is Woody Allen, really?

Alas, though the cowboy myth remains powerful, cowboys today are little more than a pair of pressed Wranglers, a hat, and a bunch of pickup truck TV commercials. ("Built Ford tough," the announcer growls, while a bale of hay the size of Rhode Island lands in a truck bed.) Cowboys are a fashion statement, a dance step, and sometimes a song.

Still, Texans hold on to the values of the cowboy: " . . . wild in a well-established tradition of Western wildness that involves drinking, fighting, fast and reckless riding and/or driving, and, of course, seducing," as McMurtry described them in *In a Narrow Grave*. Hud drives like a maniac and parks in Alva's flowerbed. When she complains, he just tells her to, "Stop plantin' flowers where I park." Here is the predecessor of the fellow I heard on the radio insisting people who drive the speed limit be banished to the service road. "I always say the law was meant to be interpreted in a lenient manner," Hud says.

Hud (which is based on McMurtry's *Horseman Pass By*), like *Giant*, is a story about a culture coming to the end of its rope, the story of the cowboy staring down the barrel of oil. Even *Lonesome Dove,* McMurtry's cattle drive epic, has a certain wistfulness, a feeling of last hurrah. Call doesn't decide to drive the cattle across the country because the cattle need moving, but because he is restless, getting too comfortable, feeling fenced in. One night he thinks, "This would have been a good night to cross some stock," and that is where the last big adventure begins.

The last significant modern pop cowboy was John Travolta in *Urban Cowboy,* and he was actually an oilfield roughneck. An "urban cowboy" is an oxymoron. "Are you a real cowboy?" the rich, sexy Houston chick asks John Travolta in *Urban Cowboy,* and he lets her believe he is. Close enough.

Wildcatters, who ushered in the era of oil, were the last generation of men who really could strut with the sexy machismo of authentic cowboys, albeit sans saddle. The wildcatter rode the range once ridden by cowboys but focused on what was under the soil rather than on it. After the wildcatter, the Texas stereotype became J.R. Ewing, who remains with us today. Perhaps the closest thing to a cowboy we have left in America is the trucker, who lives a solitary life, pushing his physical limits, moving America's product, tending to his rig, and eating greasy food.

Rodeo cowboys keep part of the culture alive: the fancy riding part and that delicious jeans and boots *je ne se quois.* Rodeos are fun "in a cultural-experience kind of way," says Anne. The scene and backstage action are the most fun: cowboys perched all in a row on a fence, like a postcard or a souvenir T-shirt; bull riders lowering themselves onto testy penned bulls; apple-cheeked blonde girls with cotton candy hair dressed up like Rodeo Barbie. It's more fun than the center-ring action. Putting broncs and calves through such painful paroxysms for entertainment, glory, and gigantic belt buckles is a little too gladiatorial for my taste. I can do a rodeo now and then, but I don't go often. Cerie tried it once. "My husband had hay fever and was so uncomfortable in his tight jeans, we never went back," she says. (Perhaps this tight jeans dilemma inspired the bucking bronco competition, in which an uncomfortably tight strap around the bronc's abdomen makes him buck.) My preferences in the rodeo arts are for the skill and speed of the chick sport of barrel racing, and bull riding, which as far as I can tell hurts the cowboy more than the creature and really is amazing to witness—more so on a real bull than on the mechanical bull made famous by Travolta and erotic by Debra Winger.

The dance floor is one place where today's cowboys remain dreamboats, dressed in crisp cotton, smelling deliciously of starch and cologne, and dancing like they have wings on their boots. You might spot cowboys on stage, too. Happily, music made in Texas has a lot more to do with cowboys than the pop pap coming out of Nashville these days. Go to the White Elephant Saloon in Fort Worth some Saturday night, and if you tilt your head and hold your breath, you'll catch strains of the true cowboy way. (It's a pity so few Texas singer/songwriters manage to break through the Nashville wall of schlock to reach a national audience. I think people all over the country could learn to love country music if they ever heard it done right.)

The cowboy mystique is sexy and cool and when it's not obnoxious, deserves to live forever, though I don't know if it can. If you drive into the sticks—the Panhandle, perhaps—you'll see guys who walk and talk like cowboys. They're out there chewing toothpicks and picking fights with Oprah. But if you live in a city like Dallas, you can practically forget they ever existed.

"You from where?" our taxi driver asked in broken English, as he negotiated the chaotic roads of Kusadasi, Turkey.

"Texas," my husband and I replied.

"Cowboys!" said the cabbie.

"Yeah," said my husband. "But the team really stinks these days."

B.Y.O.M. (Bring Your Own Meat)

"If you're having the party and you're northern it's creepy, because all of a sudden everyone's there. Where I come from, if the invitation says 7:30, you go at 8 or 9."

—Pat, Massachusetts,
seven years in Texas

*T*exans' casual style means entertaining can be low-stress and high fun. I've been to parties where the only things my hosts did was buy beer and mixers and light the barbecue. Everything else was supplied by the guests, who arrived not only with potluck for all, but with their own meat stuff to throw on the grill. When you invite people over in Texas, they will always ask, "What can I bring?" and mean it. At the very least, they will come toting a six-pack. This is the way things are done here although it took me some getting used to. I've embarrassed myself more than once by turning up at parties sans casserole dish. While my friends across America were attending church potluck suppers, I was learning at my daddy's knee (Dad could throw a helluva party) that guests should never be expected to bring their own anything. I'm learning to adapt.

My daddy's ingredients for a successful party are too much food, too much to drink, and invite twice as many people as you want because half won't show up. In specific Texas terms, that would mean lots of tortilla chips, lots of beer, and invite every-one who has ever acted like your friend because half of them probably didn't mean it anyway (see "Bless Your Heart, Aren't You Just the Most Precious Li'l Clod," page 111).

There are two good basic Texas-style parties anyone can pull off with little planning. The first is the football party, which requires little more than beer, of course, and a meal that can be eaten from a La-Z-Boy. Beans are great for this because you can cook up big pots of them and serve thousands. Your basic football party meal is a bean-based dish like chili or soup, corn bread, beer, and chips. Nachos are also good and easy. If you want to bring sentimental tears to natives' eyes, buy single serving bags of Fritos, cut them open across the front, and pour chili in. Serve in the bag. This is called "Frito Pie" and it's a high school football staple.

Speaking of beans, New Year's Eve or Day require black-eyed peas, which are eaten for luck. Unfortunately, only the most talented southern cooks (my friend Philip's mama, for example) can make black-eyed peas really yummy. If a Texan offers to bring the black-eyed peas, take her up on the offer, unless you have great faith in your culinary skills. Linda swears you can just follow the recipe on the bag of peas, but I'm skeptical. I've seen many a bowl of bland pea mush. Of course, if your black-eyed peas don't turn out perfect, don't sweat. I've been to more than one party where everyone just nibbles an obligatory pea or two for luck before returning to more palatable fare.

Barbecues are also fun and a year-round entertaining staple. Tom even smokes our Thanksgiving turkey on the grill. And men love barbecuing—not only lording over fire and searing flesh, but also the tools it requires. "I have seen grown men purchase $5,000 grills like my dad bought a mid-life crisis Miata. And then they all oo-and-ahh over it, Shiners in hand, on the back deck," says Anne. "I didn't think it was possible to spend more than a few hundred on a grill before I moved down here."

You will probably do 95 percent of the prep work for a barbecue, but when the time comes to actually transform meat into food, men will puff out their chests, grab large grilling implements, and step up to the task, while the other men stand around the grill with beers and kibbitz. It is a sad Texas chick whose husband does not consider barbecue one of the manly arts. "My husband says 'why should I stand out there where it's hot and buggy and smoky?'" my southern friend Christine sighs. "It's awful."

My husband, Yankee though he is, has embraced his role as Barbecue King. I encourage this. He's been known to take over cooking duties at other people's houses, as no one's barbecue technique lives up to his exacting standards. I'm not sure how other Barbecue Kings feel about this, but no one ever says "no" to Tom's barbecued ribs, chicken wings, steak, or salmon.

Texans have had graciousness and hospitality bred into them for many generations, and they make delightful party guests. They show up, they smile, they chitchat, they make the rounds, they can manage to make your party guests feel welcome. They don't even mind cooking for your parties and practically have to be held back from doing so. It's the rare guest who shows up empty-handed, and it's usually me.

Throwing parties in Texas is easy, and a perfectly acceptable bash can be pulled together at a moment's notice. Just keep a few staples in the house, learn a few throw-it-together dishes, and don't sweat it.

A Few Foolproof Recipes for Yankee Cooks in Texas

Yankee Tom's Frozen Margarita

1 6 oz. can frozen limeade
1 can tequila
½ can triple sec

Put ingredients in a blender, fill to the top with crushed ice, blend. We make these by the vat when we have parties. They're not fancy, but they're popular.

Linda's "I'm the non-cook" Quesadillas

"They're just fancy grilled cheese sandwiches," Linda says, "the way I do it, which I've completely made up. I don't know how they do it in restaurants.

"Heat a frying pan or griddle as you would to make a grilled cheese. Butter one side of the tortilla lightly and put it in the pan butter side down. Add sliced or grated cheese to one half. Traditionally, you use white queso cheese—redundant, I know, but that's how it's packaged. Cojack is also used. I like sharp orange cheddar best.* You can add whatever else you want: chili peppers or salsa, onions, bits of cooked chicken.** Fold the other half of the tortilla over the cheese and kind of tamp the edge together like a ravioli or pirogi. Cook till the first side is golden brown, then flip and do the other side. You can scoot it around the pan a little as it cooks if you want to be sure it browns evenly. The only thing to be careful of is not burning it and not using too much cheese and having it ooze out and burn, unless you like it that way."

* *That would make it a Yankee quesadilla.*
** *I like making these with canned black beans, onions, peppers, cumin, and cheese. It's a meal.*

Chop 'n' Serve Salsa

I'm embarrassed that it took me nearly twenty years to even attempt my own salsa when it's so darn easy. Karen from L.A., who taught me the salsa secret, likes the meditative activity of chopping by hand, but I want my salsa in a New York minute and go for small electrics.

Experimenting with proportions to taste, toss into a food processor: tomatoes, onion (red is good), fresh jalapeños, cilantro, maybe a radish or two, lime juice. Whirrrrrrrr. Salsa.

Easy Guacamole

2 small, soft avocados
1 Roma tomato, seeded and chopped
About 1/4 medium onion, peeled and chopped
Bottled salsa

Scoop out the avocado meat and mash with a fork or potato masher. Add the tomato and onion along with a couple of tablespoons of salsa, to taste. Stir until blended.

Pseudo Queso

1 lb. cubed Velveeta
1 can Ro-Tel tomatoes with chili peppers

Melt "cheese." Stir in Ro-Tel. Keep warm.

This stuff is ubiquitous. It travels well in a crock-pot and everybody loves it. "I'm not going to lie: I like it, no matter how processed it is," Maggie says.

Karen's Discover-the-Crock-pot Pinto Beans

"I have become obsessed with cooking pinto beans in my crock-pot, which I never used until I moved here," says Karen. "You buy the beans for like a dollar, wash them, take out any little stones, fill the crock-pot with water, dump in the beans and let them cook all day. I know some people* put bacon and lard and other fattening things in, but I try to keep it healthy. When they're done, I put some in a tortilla with taco sauce/salsa and some cheese."

That would be the real Texans.

Everything-but-Pancakes Grilled Poblanos

Place whole poblano peppers on the grill. When skin is blackened, pop immediately into a Ziploc bag and let steam about 15 minutes. Peel skin off with knife or fingers and slice or chop. I put these on steaks, baked potatoes, nachos, in quesadillas and omelettes—everything but pancakes. I learned this trick from my friend Jennie (or maybe it's Ginnie), who is one of the best Texas cooks I know. Any pepper can be prepared this way, but I particularly like the flavor of the poblano. If you do this to a jalapeño, you've made a chipotle.

Texas Husband's Layered Nachos

"These are truly the best nachos I have ever had and they are so easy," Joyce says. "My husband makes them every 6 weeks or so and we chow down!"

Brown about a pound of ground meat and one package of taco mix in a pan until meat is cooked. Drain and set aside. Warm a can of refried beans on a back burner while cooking meat. Optional: Add chopped white onions to beans while warming. Chop up a red onion, some green onions, and a few Roma tomatoes. Optional: Red or green peppers. Layer a cookie sheet with tortilla chips. Make sure there are no holes, overlapping chips will hold all the layers best. Spread refried beans over chips. Pour meat over refried beans. If desired, add a layer of shredded iceberg lettuce. Add a layer of red onion, then green onion, peppers if desired, tomatoes, and sliced jalapeños if desired. Top with lots of shredded cheese. Bake at 350 for 30 minutes or until warm all the way through. Let cool for 15 minutes. Cut with a knife or cake spatula and scoop out onto plates. Serve with salsa, more jalapeños, and sour cream.

Yankee Tom's Crock-pot Ribs

Two pounds country style pork ribs
Bottled barbecue sauce
Onion

Jalapeños (optional)

Salt and pepper ribs, broil in oven for 30 minutes, drain off fat. Put ribs, quartered onion, pepper if desired, and about half a jar barbecue sauce into the crock-pot and add some water. Cook all day.

Broccoli Corn Bread

Two packages Jiffy Corn Muffin Mix
One medium onion, chopped
Four eggs
One stick margarine
One cup cottage cheese
One pkg. frozen chopped broccoli, thawed and drained

Mix ingredients together and pour into a greased 9 x 12 baking pan. Bake at 375 until golden brown. Serve warm. Reheats well; great to carry to parties because it doesn't spill. I'm told this is a southern classic. I like it because it's almost like eating a vegetable, but it's not.

Mary's Toss-It-Together Taco Soup

Brown then drain 1 lb. ground beef. Put in crock-pot with 2 cans stewed tomatoes; 1 pkg. taco seasoning mix; 1 can hominy; 1 can black beans. Cook on low, adding water if needed. At the last minute, add 1 can Ro-Tel tomatoes and 1 pkg. ranch dressing mix. Serve topped with grated cheese. "Ingredients for taco soup must be kept on hand at all times," Mary says.

Your Texas Kitchen

Kitchenware You'll Want

Iced-tea jug
Big iced-tea glasses
Margarita glasses
Tortilla warmer
Crock-pot
Large cooler

Barbecue Setup

A good grill with a lid. Gas or charcoal is a matter of personal preference.
Tools, especially good tongs and a large spatula
Hickory or mesquite wood chunks
Skewers

Kitchen Staples

Tortillas: Supermarket brands are fine, or buy from tortilla companies or Mexican restaurants that make their own.

Tortilla chips: Chips and salsa are a little party all by themselves.

Salsa: For the chips, yes, but I also can no longer eat eggs without it.

Chile powder: Even if you just use to doctor a package mix.

Cumin: A key Tex-Mex seasoning.

Pickled jalapeños: Necessary for nachos, great on pizza, I even chop them into tuna fish salad.

Canned beans, black and refried: On or in tortillas, nachos, quesadillas, enchiladas, burritos. Dried beans also are great, but you have to remember to soak them.

Cheese: To glue your nachos together.

Beer: Unless you're a 12-stepper, people will think you're a little funny if you don't have at least one bottle tucked somewhere in the back of your refrigerator. In San Antonio, especially, make it Shiner Bock.

Margarita fixings: Keep tequila, triple sec, and a margarita mix or lime juice or limeade handy. (See recipe page 211.)

Packaged Shortcuts You Can Get Away With

Wick Fowler chili mix (Wick Fowler was the first Texan to package and sell his chili spice mix.)

Jiffy Corn Muffin Mix

Bisquick

Ro-Tel tomatoes and chiles

Hidden Ranch Original Ranch Dressing Mix

Wolf Brand canned chili (You probably wouldn't want to serve it in a bowl, but you could put it on nachos and not hurt anyone's feelings.)

Bottled picante sauce

Kitchen tips

- To soften tortillas, either warm in a lightly greased heavy skillet or wrap in moist paper towels and zap in the microwave about 10 seconds per corn tortilla, 15 seconds per flour. I've also heard about people warming them on the *back* of an iron skillet. Once warmed, keep wrapped in paper towel in your tortilla warmer.
- Let your iced tea cool to room temperature before refrigerating. Tea refrigerated immediately will get cloudy and may not taste right.
- Mix fresh cilantro into bottled salsa to brighten up the flavor.
- Chili powders contain mixes of ground chiles and spices. Ground chile peppers are straight chile and are available in varying degrees of heat. Cayenne is the pepper you want to heat up a package mix.
- If you eat a chile pepper that's too hot for you, don't run for water, which just spreads the oily capsaicin that gives chiles their heat. Milk or ice cream will wash away fatty capsaicin molecules; bread, tortilla, or rice also can absorb some of the oil.
- A cooler kept in the car is handy when you're running errands and can't get perishables home right away. ᕦ

Barbecue Tips

- Bring meat to room temperature before putting on the grill.
- Let your fire get nice and hot. Patience is a virtue in barbecuing.
- Don't just toss meat on and leave it because it may stick to the grill. Check it and move it from time to time, keeping in mind the grill loses heat every time you lift the lid.
- If you're using barbecue sauce, apply it late in the grilling process or it will just blacken.
- Skewers of mixed vegetables on the grill look pretty and festive, but don't do that. Different vegetables cook at different speeds. Skewer like veggies together and remove from heat as they finish cooking.

About Chile Peppers

Chile peppers are a cult icon and an entire hobby by themselves. Growing up, the only peppers I saw were bell. Here, especially at supermarkets catering to Hispanics, entire walls are given over to displays of gleaming red, yellow, and green fresh, dried, and powdered chiles. My kitchen is chile-equipped at all times. As far as my husband is concerned, if it doesn't have a chile, it's hardly food.

All you really need to know to experiment with chiles is that the seeds are the hot part of peppers. The fewer seeds you use, the milder your dish will be. So you needn't be afraid. And chiles are loaded with vitamins C and A, so you really must learn to love 'em.

The jalapeño, small, plump and green, is your basic chile pepper, good for salsa and chopping up and cooking into almost everything. My fire-eating husband likes them grilled whole. Jalapeños are also easy to grow in the ground or pots, and you'll feel like Nature Babe bringing the bounty of your garden into your kitchen. If you can also grow tomatoes, better yet— you've got two of the basic ingredients for salsa. Buy the cilantro, though. It's easier. (Or maybe it's just me.)

Peppers in general are easy to grow, though it's even easier to buy them. Poblanos and bell peppers both are meaty and grill well. Banana peppers are crisp and delicate, particularly good sliced raw into salads. Anaheim and serranos add heat to dishes. Before long, you'll be into the serious stuff, like anchos, which are dried ripe red poblanos that must be soaked before use.

Approach habanero peppers with caution. These small, round peppers, like tiny Japanese lanterns, are the hottest available. They're delicious, but in small amounts. Apparently chile scientists are trying to breed a milder habanero. That's something else they're going to blame on Yankees. ❦

Drinking Games

If you're planning a Sunday afternoon margarita party, be sure to get your tequila and triple sec by 9 p.m. the night before because you can't buy liquor by the bottle after 9 at night or on Sundays. You can, however, get a mixed drink at an establishment that serves food on Sunday—a Bloody Mary with your brunch, for example—as long as you're in a wet area. You can't get that same Bloody Mary in a bar until noon. Provided you're in a wet area, that is. If you're in a dry area, you won't be able to find a bar in which to not get your Bloody Mary. You might be able to get it before noon in a dry area if you get an inexpensive club membership from the restaurant, because it's legal to serve alcohol in private clubs in dry counties. And after 12 noon on Sunday, you not only can get your Bloody Mary any place you want in a wet area, you also can buy beer and wine, but only until midnight and if you're in a wet county.

Did you follow that?

In Texas, some counties are wet, some are dry, some places are partially wet (or partially dry, depending on your temperament). I guess Dallas County is partially dry, because it's dry in some areas and wet in others, but I'm damned if I can figure out why the boundaries fall where they do. I tried to do the right thing and research wet/dry laws for you, but the Alcoholic Beverage Code was a thousand chapters long. When I came across the following, about local elections on alcohol sales, I gave up.

(b) In areas where any type or classification of alcoholic beverages is

221

prohibited... the ballot shall be prepared to permit voting for or against one of the following issues: (1) "The legal sale of beer for off- premise consumption only"; (2) "The legal sale of beer"; (3) "The legal sale of beer and wine for off-premise consumption only"; (4) "The legal sale of beer and wine"; (5) "The legal sale of all alcoholic beverages for off-premise consumption only"; (6) "The legal sale of all alcoholic beverages except mixed beverages"; (7) "The legal sale of all alcoholic beverages including mixed beverages"; (8) "The legal sale of mixed beverages"; (9) "The legal sale of mixed beverages in restaurants by food and beverage certificate holders only."

That's way too many options. Texas liquor laws are dense and confusing and peculiar considering how much Texans like their beer. These laws, another influence of the church (the

Baptist church permits no alcohol at all), are tenacious and nobody seems to care about seeing them made more liberal except maybe restaurant owners who get caught up in them. Maria from Seattle was denied a liquor license for her sushi restaurant because the restaurant was within 10,000 feet of residences, schools, and churches. "I begged and they said they could waive the residential, they could waive the school, but there was no way to waive churches," she says.

Not having a liquor license is an economic drawback for restaurants, which is one reason dining options in my dry neighborhood are extremely limited. However, many restaurants ignore the laws and serve limited drink menus, including bellini night at one restaurant, and Samui night at the joint next door. Though I'd like more dining variety, the liquor laws otherwise don't trouble me. My husband picks up our booze on his way home from work—who really needs a liquor store down the street?

There are a zillion nuances to the codes, all locally controlled, so you'll just have to figure out your town. One hint: If you come across a sudden glut of very busy liquor stores, you are probably at the border of a wet/dry area. (The irony, of course, is that people have to drive for their booze.) Also, in wet areas you can buy beer and wine in the supermarket. Remember the no bottled-liquor-on-Sunday business; that can take the wind out of a soiree or knock it down to beer and wine. Don't try to weasel around the 12-noon thing, either. Before I knew the rules, I tried buying wine on a Sunday morning once, and the cashier took it away from me with a stern look. Some supermarkets cordon off their beer and wine sections like a crime scene. My father-in-law also was unable to persuade a waitress to serve him a Bloody Mary at 11 a.m. one Sunday. This was before the law was changed to allow booze with brunch.

I can't recall ever being refused a margarita in my neighborhood, though we have joined the faux club a few times. A couple of our favorite restaurants are BYOB, and we've been to some funky bars that have beer and wine licenses only but will sell set-ups so you can BYO hard stuff.

In other words, it's anarchy out there. But I've never seen anyone dying of thirst in Texas, so I guess it's working out OK.

The latest layer of liquor law gobbledygook is a new law permitting the sale of wine over the Internet, but only from in-state wineries, and you can't have it shipped to your home; it must be shipped to a local retailer. This would be the opposite of eliminating the middleman. But the original, more sensible, unrestricted bill first proposed was opposed by a Church of Christ minister and a beer lobbyist. When church and booze join forces, things can only get more confusing. ✦

Chapter Sixteen

That Was Then, This Is Now

"When I get homesick, I get melancholy about something that doesn't exist anymore."
Karen, Los Angeles, ten years in Texas

Watching a documentary about New York City recently, I was struck with melancholy during a segment about the Triangle Shirtwaist Factory. For the first time I understood, in a deep and resonant way, what it means to be an expatriate. The Triangle fire, a pivotal event in New York's labor history, is personal to me in a way Texas history never will be, no matter how often I hear the tales. My grandmother emigrated through Ellis Island, worked in the sweatshops, and joined the International Ladies Garment Workers Union. The Triangle fire runs in my blood. It is my history. Not so the Alamo. Though I know as much of that shrine's story, the Alamo does not touch me as the Triangle fire does and never will. (And Texans, living in a staunchly anti-union state, consider me softheaded to get misty-eyed about labor union history.) In the big picture, of course, both are American history, and we are all sisters in the eyes of the nation. But Texas, no matter how long I stay or how much I love it, will never be really mine. In *Texasville*, a grown-up Jacy who has spent much of her adult life in Europe says, "The longer I lived in Europe, the more American I felt." Exactly. It's not fatal but sometimes it chafes, like wearing a too-tight waistband too long.

Reaching my twenty-year mark in Texas, I am finding culture shock back on a slight upward curve as I become more aware of ways I might never assimilate. This culture shock is less a jolt than a low intensity buzz, or perhaps the noise in the distance that you scarcely hear until you notice it's there. In other words, although this has been my home for nearly as long as New York was, I sometimes get homesick.

When I first moved down, I declared long distance phone calls a necessary expense and did not spare it. This most immediate solution for homesickness is certainly nothing groundbreaking. Calling a Yankee friend to bitch and moan and flail and honk when you're homesick can't hurt, could help. But over the years, when "homesickness" becomes less about specifics and more about the whole gestalt of living in the two places, you might need to develop other tactics to dispel it when it hits.

I can cure homesickness with a nice long visit home. The operative word here is "long." A weekend in New York is a lot of fun. So much fun, in fact, I'm not ready to leave at the end of it. Four days is no better; that just gives me time to start thinking about where to look for an apartment and what we should sell to fit into it. After five days, though, I start daydreaming about sitting under my tree. More than a week and I start thinking that if one more person jostles me, I'll start screaming and won't be able to stop. Then it's Texas time. I adore the vitality and energy of New York, but that's an awful lot of people crammed on a tiny island. I'm not sure I could ever live like that again. New York can cure me of missing New York.

Tom's Chicago homesickness is even easier to cure. We simply plan a visit around Christmas, when winter has set in and it starts getting dark at, like, 11:30 in the morning. We have to borrow outerwear from Tom's family because we own nothing adequate, but we're never bundled enough when we're waiting for the El at night, with the wind whipping off the lake. Oh my, that's cold. We'll take Texas.

Andrea from Oregon also cites weather-related ways of dispelling homesickness. Though she often visits Oregon in its delicious summertime, "I make sure to keep reminding myself of the other nine months, when it dark and damp," she says.

Another tactic is to take a trip in Texas. Someone wise once pointed out to me that we always want to live where we vacation. Well, of course. Vacation is about indulgence, and home can be about drudgery. Yankeeland on vacation will always seem like more fun than workaday Texas. That's why a vacation in Texas will make Texas feel fun again, and fun Texas is always just a short drive away from tedious Texas. Go do something that makes you say, "Hey, cool, I'm in Texas." Go to a honky-tonk, to the Hill Country, to an auction, to a small-town festival. Go antiquing, camping, for a long, aimless drive. When I first moved down and was adjusting to the change, I adopted a picnic area on a nearby highway. It was on high ground and had long views of prairie in all directions. I drove there often after work to unwind, look at the big sky, and watch the passing cars. I even threw myself a little birthday party there once. I will never stop appreciating the great, sweeping span of Texas, though it's easy to forget when I get all crabbed up in my urban life.

If it's not too little Texas but too much that's getting you down, if you find yourself imagining you're stuck in the land of beer-drinking football morons, then seek out some sort of alternative culture, if just for an evening. Go to a punk show, an off-the-beaten-track art opening, a poetry reading, an experimental theater production. Remind yourself that these things do thrive here, even if they're not part of the dominant culture. (Nor, I hasten to add, are beer-drinking football morons. You've just been watching too many beer commercials.)

Or, bring a Yankee friend down to visit so that you are forced to show Texas off. I have a knee-jerk impulse, when

Stupid Yankee Questions

Within a month of moving to Texas, you will find yourself fielding some of the most idiotic questions you've ever heard, from Yankees back home. Prepare yourself. And don't expect them to come just out of stupid people. Some smart Yankees have some pretty stupid ideas about Texas. "My uncle who prides himself in being worldly—a lawyer, rich, owns houses in the south of France—asked if we had pizza in Texas," Andrea from Oregon reports.

Here are some real questions Yankee chicks have fielded. Think of this as a pop quiz. If any of these questions seem rational, you will require further studies.

Do they speak English?

Do they have speed limits?

Do they have trees?

I'm flying through D/FW. Can you drive up from San Antonio and meet me?

Does everyone have a horse?

Do they play just country music on the radio?

Do they have Gap/ McDonalds/Target?

Do they wear cowboy boots and hats everywhere?

Do they have any culture, like museums?

Do they celebrate Christmas?

Why do you live there?

know-nothing Yankees put Texas down, to defend it, to burst any misconceptions they may have about it. I know where they're coming from when they turn up their Yankee noses. I know how to put them straight. This always helps me convince myself, too, if I'm feeling a little wobbly. By the time I finish defending Texas, I'm in love with it again.

And I have not given up all my past life. When I'm feeling New Yorky, I can still go to my favorite deli and eat a pastrami sandwich among old Jewish ladies, even if they speak with Texas accents instead of Polish. I go to Woody Allen movies and laugh, even if I'm the only one in the theater who gets the joke, which has happened. Right now I'm on an old New York punk band kick, and I go see the old punks with New Yawk accents anytime they come through town. (And I'm finally old enough that my era is going through its revival.) On those nights, I wear all black and cuss and stay up late and smoke too much, just like the old days. Then I spend the next two days sitting under my tree feeling puny.

This sort of activity, of course, is not nostalgia for New York, but for the "good old days" in general. I occasionally have to remind myself of that. Sometimes what I really miss is the Upper West Side in the 1960s or the East Village in the late 1970s, and there's nothing to be done about that. Even lifelong New Yorkers miss that. My childhood neighborhood barely resembles what it once was, and I couldn't afford to live there, anyway.

Sometimes when I'm homesick I like public transportation, greatly improved since I did my hooker imitation on my first bus adventure. It makes me feel homey to be in transit with strangers who don't meet each other's eyes. People accuse New Yorkers of being unfriendly. I say we (they) are not unfriendly, but have lived in such close proximity with other people so long, they (we) are forced to create imaginary personal space by simply not acknowledging the humans that press so close all the time. In Texas, with all the physical space, the big houses and private cars, you don't have to invent walls. This is a good thing, but like a dog that feels secure in its crate, I sometimes like being in places where people aren't really interested in being friendly. Public transportation is like that.

I like used bookstores when I'm in a New York state of mind. There was a used bookstore in Dallas that always seemed vaguely New Yorky to me because it was dusty and crowded and un-air-conditioned. I recall one summer night browsing musty books when the smell of pizza from the restaurant next door wafted through the window, and for a brief instant I was transported back to St. Mark's Place with startling intensity.

I seek out places that remind me of home not to wallow in nostalgia, but to find the commonalities of the place I left and the place in which I live. *We have everything in Texas, we just might have only one of each.* If you miss it, seek it out. Or create it. Actually, we have a lot of everything these days. Some things you might just have to work a little harder for than you did back home or make them happen yourself. But down here, you can do that. That is one exchange we have made. We are Texans. We do not whine. We just do.

Sometimes I think staying in Texas is impossible, that I must return to my roots if I am ever to be the person I really am. Then I remember that who I am right now is nearly as much Texas as New York. And when I get back around to that point again, I throw a barbecue. With margarita in hand, meat on the grill, and friends to shoot the shit with, I'm hard-pressed to work up too much remorse for anything I left behind. Dis really is da life.